PLAYER PIANOS AND MUSIC BOXES

(KEYS TO A MUSICAL PAST)

. . . BEING AN ILLUSTRATED TREATISE ON THE VARIOUS TYPES OF MECHANICAL MUSICAL INSTRUMENTS WHICH HAVE ENLIGHTENED THE SPIRITS OF MANKIND OVER MANY DECADES, . . . WITH PARTICULAR ATTENTION PAID TO PICTURES AND ADVERTISING MATERIAL FROM THE EARLY DAYS, AND SPECIAL EMPHASIS ON THE REMARKABLE MUSICAL CHARACTERISTICS OF THESE DEVICES.

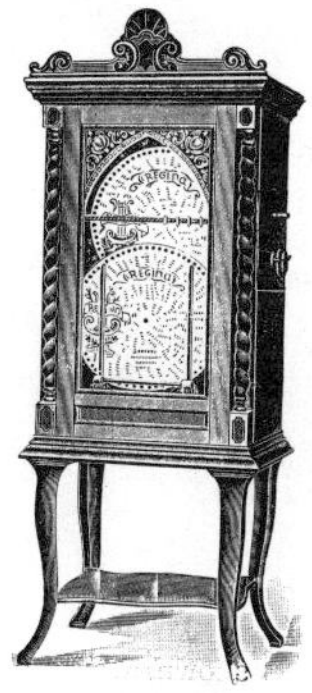

by

Harvey N. Roehl

The Vestal Press, Vestal, New York 13850

The Player Piano In America

Contents

Library of Congress Catalog Card Number 68-59054

ISBN 0-911572-06-6

First printing 5000 copies
Second printing 5000 copies

The Vestal Press Dept 51 PO Box 97 Vestal New York 13850 USA

A typical Victorian parlor of an average American home in the late 1800's. With an absolute requirement that every gew-gaw and tassle be in its proper position and thoroughly cleaned of the neat deposits of fly-ash from the ever-present soft-coal-fired pot-bellied stove (complete with mica peepholes), it's no wonder that Mother would permit occupancy only on Sunday afternoons. The reed organ, replete with unbelievable ornamentation, was standard equipment. From this atmosphere stemmed the rich tradition of automatic music in the three decades to follow.

Mention the term "player piano" to most persons and the result will be a sort of horse laugh or guffaw, as if such an instrument never served any more useful purpose than to provide amusement of a dubious character to persons of questionable intellect. But the fact is that automatic musical instruments, among them the player piano, for a period of several decades were a very serious and substantial business — on both sides of the Atlantic Ocean.

In order to gain some understanding of this, one must first re-examine the conditions that existed in the late 1800's. In a day when scientific miracles are commonplace, it's perhaps a little difficult to realize that only yesterday television hadn't been dreamed of, the radio didn't exist nor did the phonograph, electricity was pretty much of a novelty, and families were largely on their own to provide entertainment for themselves — particularly in rural America, which then constituted the largest portion of the population.

The music heard by the average family was restricted to what its members could make themselves, or if their near-by town was truly culturally oriented, what they could hear every Sunday evening in the Summer at the concert of the local town Silver Cornet band playing in the stand on Court House Square.

As the wealth of the nation and of individuals increased, more money and time became available to individuals to satisfy their musical wants, but then — as today — there was one great big catch to learning how to play a musical instrument: One had to spend a lot of time and energy to go through the learning process, and most persons simply lack the patience and the motivation to do this.

Is it any wonder, then, that there was thereby created a marvelous opportunity for clever inventors to come up with musical instruments that could be played merely by turning a crank, pushing some pedals, winding a spring, or later, dropping a coin or pushing a button? Here indeed was the chance that smart promoters had been looking for! With millions of homes eager for music of almost any kind, and with millions of persons in them anxious to sat-

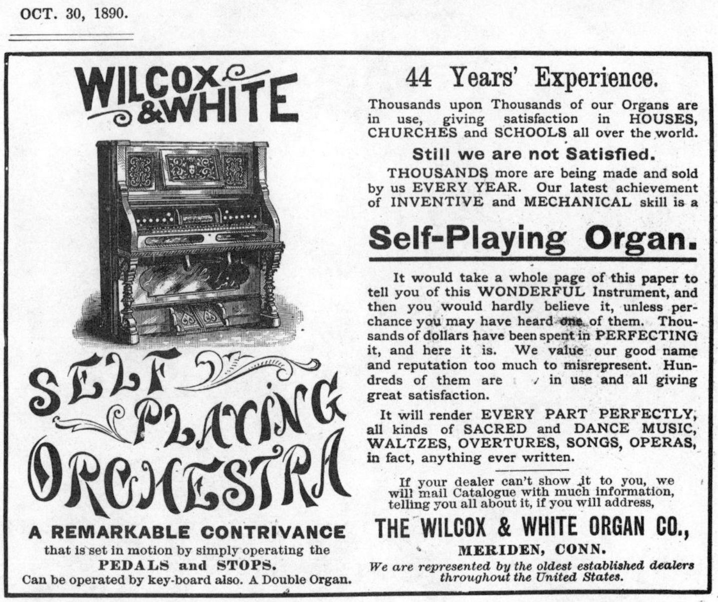

The reed organ was the first home instrument of substantial size to undergo mechanization. This Wilcox and White "Self-Playing Orchestra" was operable either by hand or by a 44-note paper music roll, and was considered a true mechanical marvel in its day — 1890!

isfy their wants with a very minimum of physical and mental effort (is it any different today?) there was created the situation about which capitalists dream! The market potential was simply enormous.

During this Victorian Gingerbread era, there were many homes which had pianos and reed organs, but generally the only person who could play either one of them was mother. The duties of rearing the children and caring for the home were such that precious little time was left for making music, so more often than not these instruments stood silent, relegated to the type of parlor shown so eloquently on page one. Of course the children, and especially the girls, were subjected to music lessons, but as is the case today few of those who start to learn ever become proficient.

Reed organs are simpler to manufacture than pianos and are therefore less costly, and thus were dominant upon the home scene during the late 1800's. It's no wonder, then, that it should have been among the first to be mechanized,

Pianos are basically more expensive to build than are reed organs, and as Americans became more affluent they began to turn more and more to the piano as the basic instrument of the home. This picture shows a typical instrument of the late 1800's, which carries much of the ostentatious decoration characteristic of the reed organ.

at least of the full-sized instruments. (We'll see later smaller table-top devices which paved the way for mechanization of both the piano and the reed organ).

The Wilcox and White "Self-Playing Orchestra" was only one of several which hit the market, and what a thrill it must have been to have been afforded the privilege of hearing one of these "remarkable contrivances", to say nothing of the sheer ecstasy which must have reigned in those homes which actually were able to have one of their very own! To sit down in front of an instrument and work the pedals as the little 44-note paper roll made the strains of "Nearer, My God, to Thee" and "Bringing Home the Sheaves" ring forth from the beautifully-ornate circassian walnut or quartered-oak cabinet was surely to bring peace to the mind of that person so privileged. Would man's wonders never cease? Was this the ultimate in God's plan?

However, then as today one scientific miracle merely begets another, and so it was with the paper-roll-played reed organ. It wasn't long before the same principles which made possible the mechanical playing of these machines were applied to devices which would play the piano.

With many homes equipped with pianos which had long stood silent, a wonderful opportunity existed for sale of playing machines which could put these instruments once more to work in providing musical entertainment. Just before the turn of the century, a whole host of these "piano players" appeared, and the one which was given the most promotion was that built by the Aeolian Corporation and called the "Pianola."

Just what basis there was for the suffix "ola" is not clear, but it managed to become clearly associated with mechanical music of all sorts, and many firms attempted to reap the harvest of popularity of this term over the years. Even today we are familiar with the "Victrola". This was the name applied originally to machines made by the Victor Talking Machine Company, and there were literally scores of other firms which worked "ola" into their product names — practically all of which are now ancient history!

Almost unknown today except in museums and private collections, piano-players were all the rage in the period from 1900 to 1905. With the distinct advantage of being able to play any piano merely by being moved to a position where its mechanical "fingers" could touch the keyboard, the music dealers really had a salable product. What home-owner would not welcome the chance to have that big upright piano in which he had invested so much money just a few years before, only to stand silent after the kids gave up their music lessons, play once more to fill the house with the latest hit tunes of the day — (and hymns on Sunday, of course)?

For about $250 one could purchase a piano player, and while in those days this represented a goodly sum of money, it was really an investment rather than an expenditure — an investment in the best interests of the cultural development of the children, to say nothing of providing an excuse to demand that they stay home evenings and soak up music rather than drift toward whatever mischief might be available elsewhere in the neighborhood.

Historians agree that the tremendous marketing effort put forth by the Aeolian Corporation in promoting the Pianola is what really set the stage for the development of the mechanical music industry in America for the next three decades. While other manufacturers were content with small ads in obscure sections of the magazines of the day, Aeolian literally staggered the rest of the industry by

The PIANOLA METHOD

IT IS a conservative statement to say that no system of piano instruction ever invented can show the results obtained by the Pianola method of playing.

Aside from the fact that in all other methods, days and years are required to perfect technique (which the Pianola supplies at once) their accomplishment is insignificant compared to the Pianola's.

Unlike that of even the most skilful pianist the Pianola-player's repertoire is practically unlimited.

Beethoven's works, arranged for the Pianola, alone form a collection greater than the whole repertoire of most players.

Add to these the compositions of practically every other composer who ever lived, of all schools, from classic to lightest popular, and the result is an enormous collection of 8,908 pieces, all instantly available for the Pianola.

When it is realized that the Pianola can be played by absolutely every one, and that its playing can not be distinguished from that of the best pianists, the tremendous advantages of the Pianola method are apparent.

To the great class of people who could never learn anything of music except by listening to the performances of others, the Pianola appeals as one of the greatest gifts science has ever conferred upon mankind.

The first five years of the twentieth century were ones of exercise of real mechanical ingenuity by musical instrument inventors, matched only by the linguistic cleverness of the advertising copy writers! In an age when true scientific marvels are commonplace, the reference in the top left ad to the Pianola as "one of the greatest gifts science has ever conferred upon mankind" rings a ludicrous note, but it was serious business in those days. Note that the ad on the right uses the term "piano player" rather than the later usage "player piano."

Theatre buffs will recognize that the lady at the upper left, evidently in a state of sheer ecstasy over the performance of the Simplex piano player, is none other than the famous Anna Held!

The difference between the Pianola and Pianola Piano is just this: In the latter instrument the Pianola is made *an integral part of the piano*, instead of being in the form of a cabinet to move up in front of the keyboard. With either instrument, the method of playing is the same; and just as successful results are attained with one as with the other. But the Pianola Piano has the obvicus advantage of *compactness*, economy of space, and it costs no more than a piano of equal grade and the Pianola when bought separately. If you already own a piano, you can turn that instrument in, applying it on the purchase of a Pianola Piano, receiving a fair allowance based upon the make, condition, etc. We specially invite correspondence relative to exchanges, and allowance estimates may be obtained without the inquirer incurring the slightest obligation to purchase. An art catalog of the Pianola Piano will be furnished upon request.

To modern-day engineers and technicians the term "miniaturization" is commonplace. The fellows who "miniaturized" the clumsy Pianola and squeezed its contents into the confines of the case of the ordinary piano never heard of the term, but they went right ahead and got the job done anyway — an accomplishment considered a miracle at the time. With this happening, the "piano player" became extinct and the "player piano" was a reality.

placing *color* ads of the most expensive sort, often running to four entire pages, in many of the most exclusive magazines. While these colored ads can't be compared with the magnificent type of graphic material we see in all types of media today, nevertheless even the tinge of color was enough to attract the attention of the reader at a time when black-and-white was the rule, rather than the exception.

The music rolls for these early playing devices were able to play 65 notes of the normal 88-note piano scale, and frequently this necessitated a re-arrangement of the original music in order to make it "fit". (mutilation might be a better word) But the important thing was that for the first time, one could bring right into the home the actual playing of some great artist of renown, through the medium of the perforated paper roll! While it might be devoid of much shading and interpretation, at least the notes were struck in the proper order and in the proper time, and this was no small feat.

The chance to be able to pedal through such hits as "Hello, Central, Give Me Heaven" and the "Maple Leaf Rag" made an impact upon the American home that is difficult for us to appreciate over half-a-century later. Manufacturers and inventors reaped a financial harvest as did music dealers; humanitarians saw a chance to bring culture to the musically deprived, educators saw the chance to bring new techniques to the musical training of the young, and composers were given new fields to conquer. Furthermore, a whole new type of job was created — that of the music-roll arranger!

But back to things mechanical. The piano players, despite their inherent musical worth, were clumsy things; they had to be carefully adjusted to play the piano keys properly, they had to moved if one wanted to play the piano by hand, and they presented one more thing to catch dust. So the builders went to work and did something that space-age scientists had to do 50 years later — they "miniaturized" the piano player, so that it would fit right inside the case of the ordinary piano! Aeolian brought their new model on the market in 1905, and this new concept caught on so well that by 1910 the "piano player" was extinct and had been replaced by the "player piano."

Now the advertising emphasis changed, and typical of the new trend is the Starr ad below, wherein it is made very clear how simple indeed it now was to make the switch from hand-playing to roll-playing. The clumsy 'push-up' device was now passe', and even a child could

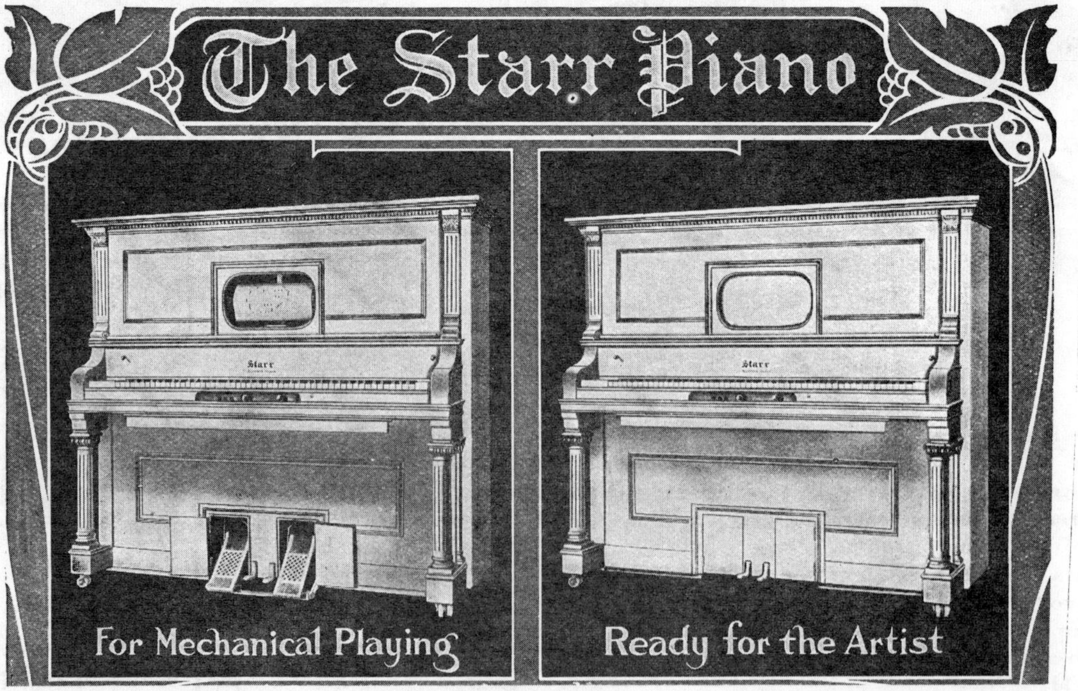

Early advertising of the player piano reflected much emphasis on the ease with which the owner could convert his instrument from hand playing to the music roll mode of operation. Most builders shied away from the term "mechanical" in their advertising, but the Starr people were slow to recognize that this wording in their ads tended to offend those persons with acute sensitivities toward musical perfection.

easily prepare the change-over. Of course it may be assumed that most pianos were set for roll operation practically all of the time; why should anyone bother with playing by hand when merely pushing the pedals would provide all the music for which anyone could ask?

Of course it's not right to imply that each and every home had a player piano. The $700 to $1,000 that these pianos cost in those days was a very large sum of money, and ownership of one was very much of a prestige proposition, to be anxiously sought in order to "keep up with the Joneses". But the advantages of cultural enlightenment for the children was not to be overlooked, and many was the family which scrimped and saved and did without other worldly goods that the family might have the benefit of one of these marvelous pieces of apparatus.

One of the most interesting aspects of the whole era of mechanical music was that of the promotional efforts behind it. With a surge of music-in-the-home type of interest on the part of the general public never before experienced, those dealers who were quick to grasp the potentialities of the situation pulled out every stop to make the best of this new market.

For example, take the "demonstration". Just as in earlier days automobile dealers were anxious to take their cars right to the potential buyer's home and let him "try" the car, aggressive piano dealers took pianos right to the front yards of prospective customers! In those days almost everyone had a Ford car or roadster, and firms such as Atwood or Bowen built devices which would make it an easy trick to whip the piano right out to one's home merely by swinging the instrument onto the back of the vehicle. Dealers weren't content to wait until the prospect wandered into the showroom; they went right out and got 'em!

Naturally, it took a good instrument to stay anywhere near in tune during the jouncing ride along the rutted unpaved roads of the day, but if it did, then all the more ammunition was added to the sales talk of the peddler! It might not be nice to suggest that probably most pianos didn't really hold their pitch very well with this treatment, and that perhaps most player-piano buyers just weren't very discriminating in their tastes. But these and other techniques got the instruments into the homes, put music in the ears of the owners, and put money in the pockets of the dealers, the builders, and the music-roll cutters and arrangers. Hopefully, happiness was brought into the homes as well!

The men who wrote the advertising for these pianos used every trick in the book, and compared against the sophisticated Madison avenue techniques of today, many seem pretty corny. But they worked, and this is what keeps factories running and workers employed.

This cartoon evidently is from the period when player piano ownership was a goal which was sought eagerly by every family. The heartless deception of the maid seems almost too much for a human being to bear.

HER KICK.

"Why do you wish to leave, Marie. Haven't you had your two days and Sunday off and your two nights for company, with use of the parlor and piano and——"

"That's the answer. The employment agent said you had a playerpiano, but he deceived me."

ONE MAN—THE SALESMAN—LOADS, GOES WHERE HE PLEASES, SHOWS PIANO TO EVERY PROSPECT, AND USUALLY RETURNS WITH THE CASH

THE BOWEN LOADER—Makes Every Call a Demonstration

More sales are made when your salesman actually shows the goods. With a Bowen Loader and a Ford Roadster he can travel anywhere—reach the prospects who can't or won't come to your store. Price reduced to $95, including an extra fine waterproof moving cover.

Fully Guaranteed. ***Shipped to Responsible Dealers on Approval.***

BOWEN PIANO LOADER CO. **WINSTON-SALEM, N. C.**

Remember the days when automobile dealers would bring cars to your home for you to "try?" Piano merchants peddled player pianos by the hundreds of thousands all over the land by this technique, but today we have to pack up and go to *their* air-conditioned showrooms to have the advantages of the particular brand of merchandise explained.

When player pianos were big business, even large highway billboards were brought into the merchandising act.

It was important for the public to know that playerpianos could withstand extremes of climate and other operating conditions. Service on battleships and polar expeditions proved beyond a doubt the durability of this particular make!

From baby-sitting to entertaining polar explorers to amusing the sailors and marines, player pianos were everywhere and the ad-writers made certain that the public knew about it. They certainly tried to make it crystal-clear that no self-respecting home could possibly do a proper job of raising a family without a player piano at hand to do its part, and about the only aspect of life not covered in the "Heart Appeal of Music" advertisement is that of the funeral dirge. (Why they left this out is not clear, but it is interesting to note that paper-roll-operated small pipe organs were a prominent fixture in most undertaking establishments during this period). Undoubtedly the reasoning here was that the positive aspects of life should be emphasized, with the idea of getting across the message that one could not possibly have a full, rich devoted family life without a player piano in constant attendance.

This particular series of pictures appeared in a beautifully-printed four-color booklet, to be handed to prospective customers by piano dealers. It was put out by the Standard Pneumatic Action Company, which built player mechanisms for sale to piano manufacturers, to be installed in their instruments. The "Dear Ann" letter is from a series of ads by the same concern called "The Confidences of Betty", wherein a mythical "Betty" makes subtle suggestions to her friends about the absolute necessity of a player-piano in the home for proper child-rearing.

Could there be any more compelling argument in favor of the player piano than to associate it with motherhood? This touching advertisement makes it quite clear that here, indeed, was the solution to every mother's prayer for help in attending her young.

THE HEART APPEAL OF MUSIC

Jim has invited his college friends over.

Music,-To suit her hour of romance.

The first Lullaby is sung to the Babe in arms.

"See, Mother! I can play."

Give them Song and Dance and Happiness.

That song we used to sing before we were married.

She is playing "Home, Sweet, Home."

The life-cycle of the player piano, or rather the life-cycle of homo sapiens with player piano. As if to suggest that it would otherwise be biologically quite impossible for a family to go through its course from one generation to another, this heart-warming advertisement (originally prepared in four colors) traces an entire series of events from young manhood, courtship, parenthood, childhood, growing-up, recollections, and grandparentcy — all to the rhythm of the perforated paper music roll!

The Literary Digest for March 3, 1923

Evidently the QRS people recognized that too many persons were not learning to play the piano by hand, and this might be the source of future difficulty. The QRS Educator Set of 6 music rolls was designed to alleviate this problem. It sold for $11.50 in 1923, and was not a commercial success.

This type of advertising was considered pretty clever in the promotion of player pianos, and it moved a lot of instruments. Unfortunately, it was also short-sighted, as an entire generation of Americans slighted the opportunity to learn to play by hand. This in turn caused a severe depression in the piano industry one generation later, after the popularity of the player had waned. The Gulbranson Baby and the Victor Dog are probably the two most famous trade-marks in mechanical music.

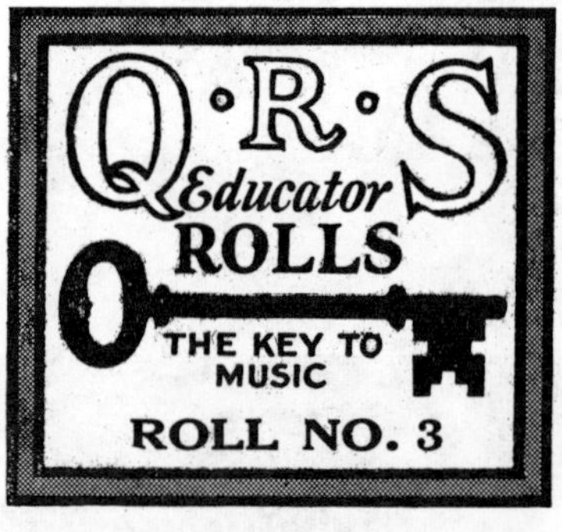

In the 1960's there was a great flurry of interest in "teaching machines" and "programmed instruction" in the schools and colleges. The player piano people got the jump on them 40 years earlier with these rolls, but apparently the public was not ready to accept the idea at that time.

The extent to which the merchandisers of player pianos succeeded in their efforts is revealed in the chart at the right. During the 30-year period of the rise and fall of popularity of this type of instrument, some 2½ million of all types were built in America. It's interesting to note that the greatest rise in interest was during the 1917-1918 World War I period; many collectors today specialize in the music of that period. The peak sales year was 1923, and after that sales really dropped.

It was during the early 1920's that the phonograph really started to amount to something, and of course radio was just being introduced. As is always the case, the public quickly changed its allegiance to newer mediums of home entertainment. Piano trade papers during this period are interesting to read, as one manufacturer after another would assure his dealers that their falling sales were nothing that couldn't be rectified by more hard work, etc. etc. . . . but the handwriting was on the wall, and by 1930 the player industry was dead. Some builders had tried to stem the tide by installing radios and phonographs right inside the pianos together with the player mechanisms, but this idea never caught on and these instruments are merely rare historical curiosities today, again showing that simple gadgetry in itself cannot control the mood and tastes of the public.

While disciples of the industry were frequently hailing the player-piano as a wonderful device for the interest it would develop in youngsters to learn how to play it themselves, the fact is that this type of logic simply did not prevail. Because one no longer had to bother to learn to play "the old-fashioned hard way" (as one manufacturer put it) very few were willing to put forth this effort. After all, why should they?

This type of logic got the piano industry into trouble, although not until a generation later when it became apparent that altogether too few persons knew how to play the piano. By that time the players were gone from the homes, and the country's piano teachers had to motivate youngsters to learn not from hearing their parents play, but from hearing and seeing artists such as Liberace on television!

One of the most interesting aspects of the entire player piano industry is that of the music roll manufacturing and sales. There was no shortage of gimmickry in this field; one of the most interesting ones was actually a very reasoned approach to the problem of teaching music. These were the "Educator" rolls, put out by the QRS organization, then located in Chicago.

PRODUCTION OF ALL TYPES OF PLAYER PIANOS IN THE UNITED STATES, FROM 1900 to 1931

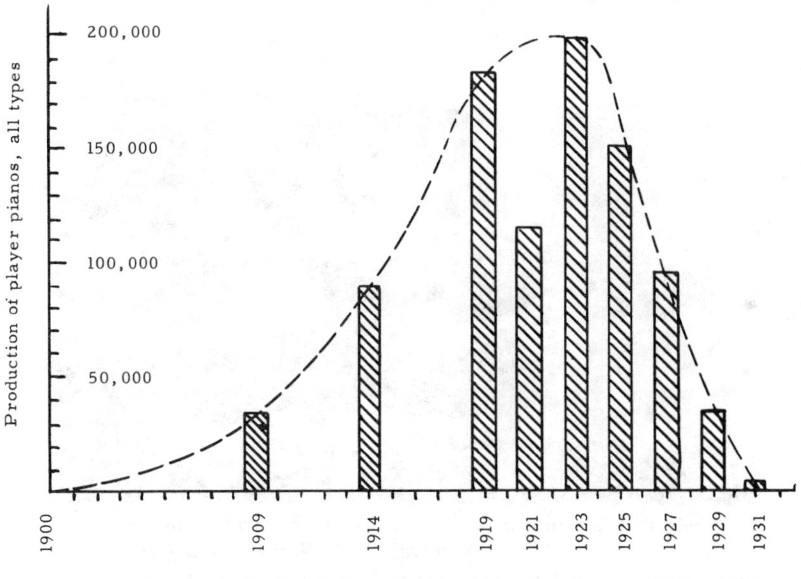

The curve represents the level of popularity of the player piano; total production in this period was about 2,500,000 machines of all types. The drop in production in 1921 was a result of the post-World-War-One business recession. Source: U.S. Department of Commerce.

The rise and fall of the player piano is clearly shown here to have happened within a 30 year period. Starting in 1900, sales moved slowly but increased rapidly during the World War 1 period, then rapidly plummetted to nothing in 1930. The fast decline is generally attributed to the increase in popularity of the radio and the phonograph.

These rolls had printed on them the correct positions of the hand and fingers to play various notes and chords, and had immediately following the perforations which would cause the piano to play those notes. Following this would be the musical staff, plus any explanations required. Sold as a set of 6, this was actually an early example of what educators today call "programmed learning"; the player piano acted as a "teaching machine." Unfortunately, the idea never caught on, even though expensive full-page magazine ads in such papers as the Literary Digest were used to herald the development of this new scheme.

Another set of interesting rolls were the "Minstrel" ones put out by the Vocalstyle Company. These contained the music and words of a short minstrel performance, the idea

Then, as today, the small dealer had a difficult time competing with the giants of merchandising. The Supertone roll was sold by Sears, Roebuck and with these low prices they must have moved a lot of them. "Word rolls" had the words to the music printed on the paper, so that the playerpianist and his friends could sing right along with the music.

Music roll arranging is accomplished by various methods. In this case, Doug Roe of the QRS Music Roll Company arranges, edits, and punches directly from a piece of sheet music to a "master roll" at the right, which in turn is used on production machinery to make up to 30 duplicates at one cutting.

being that the piano player and his friends would gather 'round the piano, sing the music, act out the little skits printed thereon, read the fantastically bad jokes printed in the little booklet that came with each roll, and then howl with laughter, slap thighs, and otherwise regale themselves at the humor of the situation! These rolls are much desired by collectors today.

The manufacture of music rolls is a process about which many persons wonder. There are a variety of ways in which this can be accomplished, but probably the greatest number made have been arranged "mathematically." This is to say that a musician examines the musical score of the piece he wishes to commit to perforations, and then makes pencil marks on a long piece of heavy paper to coincide with the

Scene in a modern player roll factory. This picture taken in 1968 shows some of the machinery in the QRS factory in Buffalo, New York. This is the one firm which, although under three different managements, has manufactured music rolls continuously since the early days of the player piano.

Music roll paper must have quite a list of special properties to be satisfactory for its purpose. It must not absorb too much moisture, and it cannot be susceptible to stretching. It must be able to be punched "clean" and not leave a lot of fuzz around the holes. It obviously has to be strong in the lengthwise direction, and these two chaps are making a vivid demonstration of the excellent strength characteristic of the material used for rolls on the European Imhof and Mukle instruments.

The best proof of the durability of the Music Rolls!

notes to be played. The length of the marks determines the length of the playing of the notes, and the position of the marks determines the note to be played. When he is satisfied that everything is correct, a punch and hammer are used to make holes where the lines are located, and the heavy long paper then becomes a "master roll". Corrections are generally necessary, of course, but basically this is the roll which is placed upon a machine which then grinds out many duplicates, which are then spooled and sold to the public.

Obviously with this method of arranging it is easy to make the piano play many more notes than could ever be operated by a human musician, and this is generally the intended result! Of course many music rolls were "hand-played", and in order to do this an artist plays a piano to which are connected a whole bank of pencils or other marking devices which can record on a moving strip of master roll paper the actual notes that are struck. These pencil marks are then punched by hand, and a master roll is created.

In the old days of piano roll manufacture, entire departments of factories were organized to perform the various

As in every other field of merchandising, someone will bring out a product absurdly cheap. How it could have been possible to manufacture music rolls for a retail price of 10¢ is certainly not clear, and it's even less clear how they could have been any good!

The Acme Music Roll Perforator is the perfected result of years of experimentation and practical manufacturing experience. Only the best materials and finest workmanship are employed in building these machines; insuring years of satisfactory service in daily operation. They are operated by unskilled labor. Some plants employ girl operators.

It perforates sixteen (16) sheets at one time at a speed of from three to six feet per minute depending upon the style of perforating desired. In other words, from 48 feet to 96 feet of music roll per minute. The sheets are trimmed to correct width as the notes are being perforated.

The Acme Perforator is unequalled for economy of operation, speed, simplicity, accuracy and quality of perforating.

Machines are furnished for perforating any standard or special music roll.

The complete machine as shown in Plate 4 weighs approximately 1600 pounds cased.

The ACME perforator was sold to music roll manufacturers. Since there were perhaps 50 concerns in this business at one time in America, a large number of these machines must have been produced.

functions — editing, arranging, correcting, and punching. In this day and age, however, all of these jobs must be accomplished by fewer people. At the factory of the QRS Music Roll Company is a special piano which permits the arranger to sit right at the instrument, develop his chord formations and timing, and punch a master roll measure by measure and then play it back for possible correction.

There is a great temptation for player piano owners to wish to make some of their own music rolls, and the Leabarjan perforator was designed to take advantage of this desire. Any one who has tried it, however, quickly learns that it is a long, tedious process, but in spite of this these machines are eagerly sought by collectors.

From the days when perhaps 50 companies were busy in America pounding out music rolls, in 1968 there are three; one other is in Australia and still another makes them in England. Of the three in America, only the QRS Company has been in continuous operation since the early days of the industry; it had its start in DeKalb, Illinois, and has since been located in Chicago, New York City, and Buffalo, New York, under three different managements. In the hey-day of the player piano it also had factories in San Francisco, Toronto, and in Holland to add to the perfectly enormous output of the industry in general!

No figures exist to tell the number of piano rolls which were manufactured in the first thirty years of the twentieth century, but it certainly must have been in the hundreds of millions.

But what of the future? Can we expect player pianos ever again to come into vogue?

Actually, they already have, to a limited degree. In 1956 the Hardman Peck Company of New York City test marketed a player piano with modern styling, and called it the Hardman "Duo" (suggestive of the dual means by which it could be played — by roll or by hand). Evidently the reasoning was that more money was in the hands of the public to spend on leisure activities than ever before, and in this environment perhaps some could be sold for use in clubs, game rooms, and the like. This reasoning proved to be correct, for sales were quite good, and as a result a number of other firms jumped into the market. As this text is written, perhaps 8 or 9 makes now are available to the American public, with total numbers around 8 or 9 thousand being sold annually.

But to suggest that these interesting musical instruments will ever gain the type of popularity they once had is simply not realistic; when it was popular, the player piano had a

MAKE YOUR OWN MUSIC ROLLS

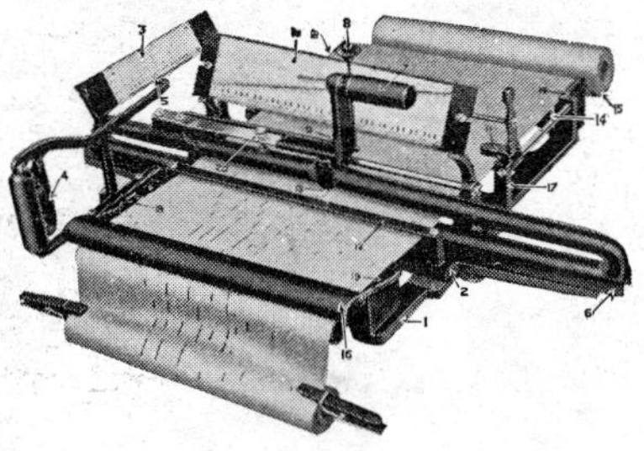

You can cut any roll your customer wants and you need not disappoint anyone. Or you can sell the **Leabarjan Player Roll Perforator** to any owner of a Player Piano.

THE LEABARJAN PERFORATOR IS A MONEY MAKER FOR THE DEALER.

It is not a toy. It is a "Full-Grown", Practical Music-Roll Maker. It will do the work quickly and perfectly, and it is the Greatest Musical Educator of the Day.

We want Agents Everywhere and will send Particulars on Request. Don't miss the Opportunity if your territory is still open. Write and see.

LEABARJAN MFG. CO., HAMILTON, O.

Imagine the tedious process of punching out your own music rolls, one hole at a time! This ingenious "home" perforator was sold for this very purpose. Whether any great number of rolls were ever made this way is certainly open to question.

In a time when people were less concerned with air pollution than are we today, a sure sign of prosperity was to have great clouds of smoke belching forth from factory chimneys. What better portrayal of the success of the Autopiano Company than this advertisement illustrating the smogging of the skies over New York City?

There was no shortage of clever artwork in the advertising and promotional efforts made on behalf of the player piano. These musical bellhops with their music-roll drum beaters seem to be having the time of their lives!

monopoly in the home musical entertainment field while today it must compete with television, radio, hi-fi, and all the rest. So it seems destined to remain a novelty for those persons who have spare cash, and who long for a little nostalgia.

Alas, then, we will not again see the day when such names as TECHNOLA, AERIOLA, AUTOTONE, COMBINOLA and INTERIOLA grace the parlors across the land and fill the advertising pages of our newspapers and magazines. Nor will such grammatical gems as PIANAUTO, AUTO-PLAYER, AUTO-GRAND, PIANISTA, or AUTOPIANO flow from the pens of Madison avenue advertising copy writers. Nor will names like AUTOLA, AIR-O-PLAYER, CONCERTONE, VIRTUOLA, MANUALO, or DULCITONE be on the minds of mother and children, as they anxiously await the day when father will have saved enough money to bring home the marvelous player piano bearing that trade-mark. And it's too much to expect that, what with the sophisticated thoughts pervading the minds of those responsible for modern-day marketing schemes, that we'll ever again see a RESOTONE, a TONE-OLA, an AERO-TONE, a STERLITONE, a SYMPHOTONE, a SYMPHONOLA . . . nor should one be looking too anxiously for the likes of a PLAYOLA, a MARVEOLA, a PURE-A-TONE, a PLAYOTONE, a PRIMATONE, a PLAYAPIANO, a WONDERTONE, a VACUOLA, a SOLOTONE, a MELL-O-TONE or a PLAYERNOLA!

In 1956 the Hardman Peck Company of New York City decided to "try" the market for a new player. Much to everyone's surprise, sales were quite good, and since that time a number of other firms have jumped back into the business. As this is written, perhaps 7 or 8 thousand player pianos are being built yearly in America as a result of the success of the "Hardman Duo" model shown above. Technically, this piano is the same as those built 40 years earlier, but its modern decor better suits the homes of today.

These all seem terribly "corny" today, but these were the names of player pianos which were sold in tremendous quantity and variety during the first 30 years of the Twentieth century, and they filled the homes of America with laughter at the funny songs, patriotism as the World War I tunes were pedalled through, pathos at the "story" rolls of tender love scenes, humor with their renditions of minstrel antics, and romance as the popular ballads of the day were sung by eager lovers. It was a never-to-be-repeated era, and as one examines the activities of those days, it's pretty difficult not to think that perhaps there was merit in life being less complicated and moving at a slower pace than it does today. . . . to the tune of the perforated music roll.

Is it any wonder, then, that the few remaining player pianos of the old days are eagerly sought by collectors and others who simply enjoy this old-time style of music, and who will put forth no end of effort to rebuild them so that once again their melodic outpourings will grace the land and delight all those who come within hearing? To those whose nostalgic interests easily overcome practical realities, no amount of effort is too much to preserve this magnificent musical heritage!

History is not clear on where credit should go as to the basic invention of the player piano. John McTammany, a veteran of the Civil War between the States, went to his Canton, Ohio grave proclaiming that the honor was rightfully his, and that others had merely stolen his ideas. Whether his claims were justified or not will never be known, but there is no doubt that he made important contributions to the art.

Music Boxes and Roller Organs

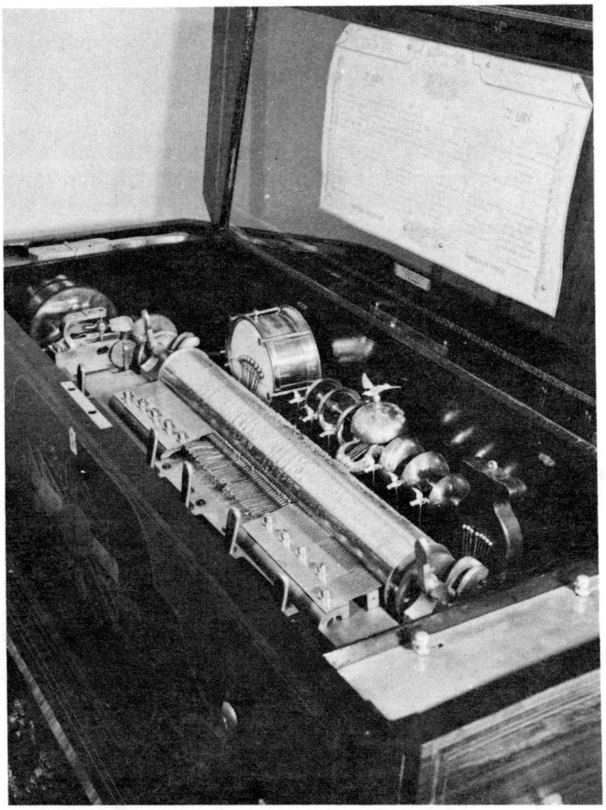

Cylinder-operated music boxes such as this Swiss Bremond machine were obviously only for the homes of the wealthy. This magnificent specimen with its beautiful matching cabinet has organ, flute, bells, drum, and castanet accompaniment to the music of the steel combs and is truly a joy to behold. ***(Photo courtesy of Mrs. Ruth Bornand, Pelham, N. Y.)***

This beautiful little snuffbox from the early 1800's is only 3¾" x 2½" x 1", and plays two tunes! Note the beautiful artwork on the cover. ***(from Musical Boxes, by E. T. Clark)***

The cradle of the history of automatic music was Switzerland, in the middle 1700's, and it came about because Swiss artisans who worked at watchmaking turned their skills toward perfection of tiny devices inside watch-cases which were capable of producing melodies. These intricate mechanisms made music — of an extremely limited character — by having pins set in tiny revolving discs strike against steel prongs of varying length. The ability of these craftsmen to do this intricate work is just as remarkable today, in spite of two hundred years of scientific advances, as it was then!

Following the customs of the day, much work was done in small shops under a cloak of secrecy as to methods employed, so much of the early history of the period is vague. Fortunately, Louis Jaccard, who was born in 1861 in Switzerland and who spent his life in the music box business put together an article entitled "The Origin and Development of the Music Box", which appeared first in Hobbies Magazine and later as a reprint of the Musical Box Society, so certain important dates are available through his researches. Also the work of John E. T. Clark of London is valuable in reviewing the early days of the business, and his book *Musical Boxes* is considered to be authoritative in the field.

The machinery inside a tiny 2″ x 3″ snuff box, dating from the late 1700's. ***(from the collection of Mr. and Mrs. Clarence Fabel)***

Jaccard tells us that Geneva, Switzerland became the center of this activity, and that most of the early efforts were directed toward placement of small musical movements in watches, seals, cane tops, jewelry boxes, and snuff boxes. The latter became extremely popular, and were produced in considerable numbers — many with cases of extreme beauty of design and craftsmanship, using precious stones and metals.

During the first two decades of the 19th century, the cylinder music box came into being. In these machines tiny metal pins are fastened at right angles to the surface of a metal cylinder, such that when the cylinder is revolved past a series of shaped teeth on a steel "comb" a tune will result. It is obvious from the inspection of even a small instrument of this type that the workmanship required to build such a device must be of a high order to get it to work at all, much less play a complicated piece of music!

This photo of a Swiss music box from the Shackleton collection shows clearly the method of producing the music. Tiny pins carefully placed to agree with the tune to be played project from the metal cylinder. As the cylinder revolves, the pins strike the carefully-tuned teeth of the metal comb, thus creating the music. It can well be imagined that the difficulty of manufacturing these pinned cylinders made high-quality music boxes of this type very expensive indeed.

We also know from the work of these historians that most of the larger music boxes and the ones with elaborate extra features were produced after 1850, notably those with reed organ devices to add an organ effect to the music, the interchangeable cylinder box which permitted the owner to have a greater variety of musical selections at his command, the boxes with bells and tiny drums with their rhythmic accompaniment, as well as the complex "revolver" boxes which held three or more cylinders in a magazine arrangement for instant change from one to the other.

A class of music box which is especially desired by collectors is the "overture" box, which were built with cylinders some 5 inches in diameter, and which had large numbers of teeth cut into their combs. Clark tells us: "The manner of setting up overtures on these large cylinders was a marvel of the arranger and cylinder prickers' art.

No. 500½.

This music box, manufactured by Mermod Freres, sold for $337.50 with a mahogany case around the turn of the 20th century. With an oak case, it was $12.50 less! Extra music cylinders of 6 tunes each were available for $45 each; a large sum in those times.

INTERCHANGEABLE CYLINDER MUSICAL BOXES.

MOVEMENT OF THE PEERLESS FORTE-PICCOLO.

Some cylinder boxes were built with interchangeable cylinders, so the owner could have more than just what tunes came with it originally.

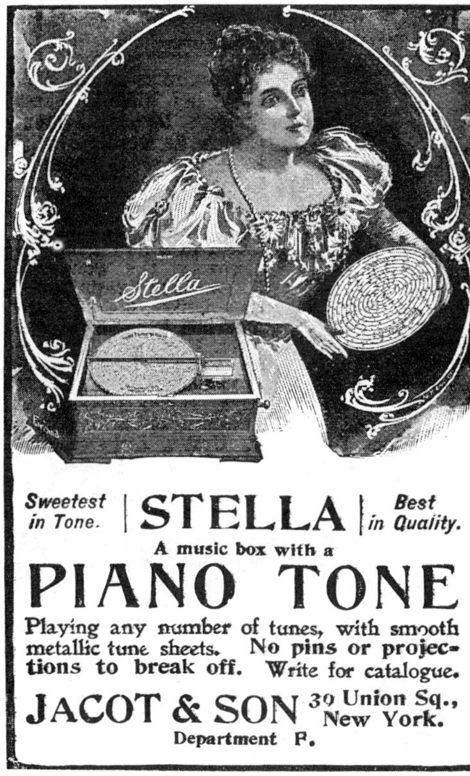

The invention of the disc-operated music box spelled the death-knell of the cylinder operated boxes, simply because discs were easy and inexpensive to manufacture. Note the emphasis in the Regina ad on the fact that it could play "1,000 tunes" — an obvious dig at the Swiss-type box which would permit few, if any tune changes. Note also the price range of $7 to $70 — truly a "breakthrough" in selling prices which would soon permit music boxes to be seen in modest homes where cylinder boxes could never have been afforded.

Short overtures such as Mozart's *Magic Flute* and Bellini's *Norma* were reproduced in their entirety and were note perfect in every way. The close-cut three and four-air combs that were made for the 20 to 22 inch long cylinders had between 300 and 400 teeth, and thus every instrument in the orchestra was able to be represented, and the passage faithfully rendered."

Now the fact that most music boxes appear to be beautiful does not mean that all are; economics worked the same way in those days as it does today, and many cheap boxes were built in order to meet price competition. For this reason any person setting about to purchase a music box would do well to study the available literature on them, learn much of what there is to know on them, and where there is doubt as to the quality of a potential purchase, to make the purchase through a reliable dealer — of which there are many throughout North America and Europe.

One of the most attractive aspects of the better class of music box is the casework. Some of the art work, the carving, and the metal and rare-wood inlay work is simply hard to believe in a day and age when just about everything is mass-produced; the Bremond instrument on page 15 and the Mermod Freres on page 16 are excellent examples of this type of craftsmanship which today is for all practical purposes a lost art.

Beautifully-feathered singing birds were a real novelty type of music box. These birds move their heads and beaks and actually chirp songs, by means of spring-driven cam-controlled whistles in the bottom of the cage. Originals bring high prices, but duplicates are being made in Europe today.

THE RUDOLPH WURLITZER CO

Singing Birds

Automatic, with Lever or Coin Slot Attachment

The Birds are Life Size, with Plumage of Natural Colors—a Very Fine Attraction.

Although Singing Birds have been on the market for years, it is only lately that they have been perfected, so that they are now a practical commercial article. Our Singing Birds have a newly perfected spring movement mechanism that is very durable. In public places these birds prove a great attraction, besides being big money-makers. Equipped with nickel-in-slot attachment, they have earned as high as $10.00 in one week.

No. 3235 No. 3236

No. 3235—Mahogany and gold brass cage; height, 18 in.; width, 10 in.; depth, 8 in. PRICE, $65.
No. 3236—Burnished gold cage, very handsome; height, 20 in.; width, 9 in.; depth, 9 in. PRICE, $75.
No. 3237—Same as 3236, but with two birds. PRICE.................................... $90.
No. 3238—Same as 3236, but with three birds. PRICE.................................... $105.
No. 3239—Same as 3236, but with four birds. PRICE.................................... $120.

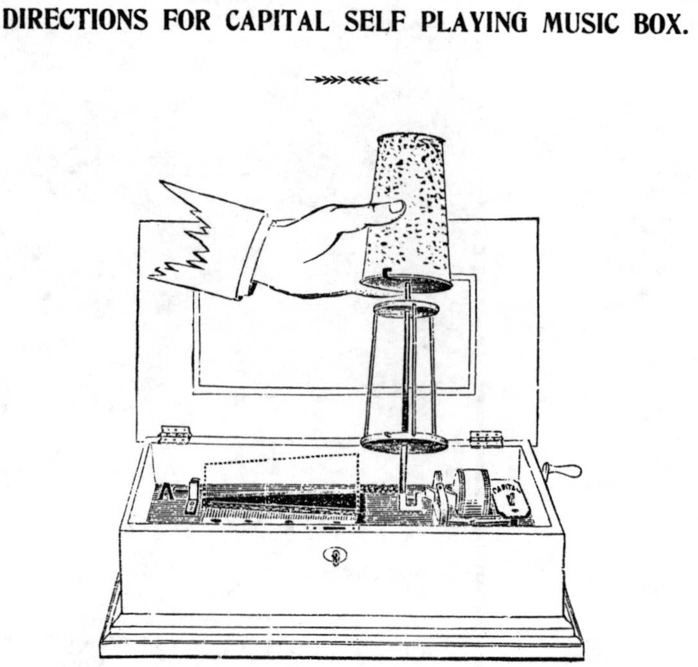

The Capital "Cuff" music box was so named because of the resemblance of the sheet-metal music cones to shirt cuffs. These machines were built in New Jersey for a short period around the turn of the 20th Century. They work in a manner similar to Swiss cylinder-type boxes, but the music was cheap and easy to manufacture, and easily interchanged. ***(From the Haning and White collection)***

The Regina music box about which the children are dancing was one of a variety of models, but none are more cherished today among collectors than this one because of their outstanding tonal qualities. It used the 15½" tune sheet, and featured an automatic changing device. The ad writer had a lot of fun with this one; note his reference to a "rattling good" Regina story, and the concept that the tune-changing device would "save all trouble."

Some of the early snuff-box movements were modified in what are known as "singing-bird boxes", wherein when the lid was opened, a tiny bird perhaps less than 3/4 of an inch in length would pop out, chirp a song, move its beak and body, and then pop back inside the case. In order to provide the chirping, it became necessary to provide tiny clock-work-driven bellows to produce compressed air, which in turn was fed to slide whistles whose pitch was controlled by rotating cams. The cams were contoured such that their outline was in accordance with the tune to be produced. Later bird boxes were made in the form of bird cages, with the creatures being encased in real feathers instead of mere ceramic or metal; in the more elaborate models these cages contained several birds with different songs according to their species! Bird boxes of this type are manufactured even today.

As the 19th century went along and more and more persons gained the financial means to spend a little of their wages on amusements, this created a market potential which made the disc-type music box an instant success. It is quite obvious that a Swiss cylinder-type music box did not lend itself to mass production; this meant that all such instruments of any reasonable degree of quality were and would always be expensive. The invention the music disc, wherein projections on a thin metal disc could be made to actuate the teeth of a comb by means of a rotating "star wheel" mechanism for the first time put the music box within reach of almost everyone. The discs were simple and easy to manufacture, as they could be stamped out almost like cookies in great quantity, and the ease by which they could be interchanged meant that for the first time an owner of this type of box could have an almost unlimited selection of music at his command. Note the Regina ad which says that their box "Plays 1,000 Tunes"!

ORCHESTRAL CORONA No. 34.

This instrument has a piano sounding board, changes the tune discs automatically, and has a long-running movement. It has two large combs with 175 tongues, embracing over seven octaves. Tune sheets are 27 inches in diameter. The case is either in oak or mahogany, highly polished. It stands 75 inches high, is 39 inches wide, and 24 inches deep.

The ***largest*** and ***best*** instrument of its kind ever made.

Without question, the greatest music box ever built in terms of sheer size is the Regina 27 inch changer model. This refers to the diameter of the music sheets, and the fact that the machine would pull them from their storage magazine, play each one in turn, and return them to the magazine. It certainly must have been considered a miracle of modern technology when it appeared!

This little hand-operated organ is typical of literally hundreds which appeared on the American market in the late 1800's. People were hungry for music in the home, and this is one way they could get it cheaply and easily, long before there was any other inexpensive way of reproducing music automatically.

The first disc music boxes came from Germany, and one Paul Lochmann gets credit for having introduced it with the trade-name Symphonion — a name which soon was seen all over the World as these new types of machines gained popularity. The German Polyphon Music Works also got into the act, as did others, and it wasn't long before it became obvious that the cylinder-box had become obsolete for the simple reason that it couldn't compete in the market-place. The Swiss-made Stella, the Mira, the Britannia and others joined the fray, and until the player piano and the radio and phonograph combined forces to turn the interest of the public away from music boxes as a type of entertainment, the factories were hard-pressed to meet the demands for the products.

The best-known American box was the Regina, built in Rahway, New Jersey by Gustave Brachhausen who came to this country in 1889 to found it, based on his experience as a partner in the Polyphon works. The Regina was an immediate success; it is said that around 1895 the company's sales were on the order of $2,000,000 each year, and that a total of some 80,000 instruments were made until the firm's demise some 30 years after its founding.

Brachhausen invented the automatic disc-changing music box, and it was an immediate success. Available in several sizes, his 27-inch-diameter-disc machine was the largest music box ever built in any quantity, and it received wide acclaim. Almost any music boxes are considered collector's items today; the large "automatic changer" is one that is considered extremely desirable because of its unique mechanical features, and the loud volume of tone.

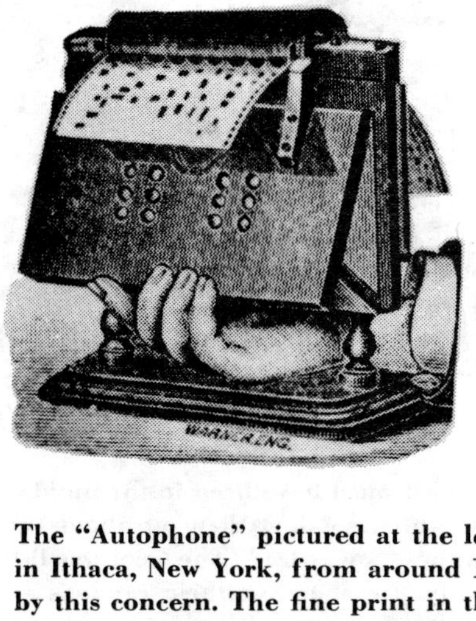

$5. The Wonderful Mechanical Piano-ette. $5.

The most marvellous mechanical invention of the age. It will play any tune in a melodious and pleasing manner. Difficult and simple music produced in a masterly style, and it can be played by a child as well as by a grown person and will furnish music for social gatherings of any description, playing hour after hour, without any knowledge of music being required in the operation. The most wonderful of all musical inventions; a machine which in a purely mechanical manner produces any kind of music, Waltzes, Polkas, Marches, &c., &c., without any practice or knowledge of music whatever; in this respect far superior to any music-box, for there is no limit whatever to the number of tunes it will play. The perforations in a flexible strip produce the effect. It has just been perfected (the accompanying cut showing it in its improved form), and is having the largest sale ever obtained by a musical instrument in the country. It has fine black walnut cases, highly decorated, the notes or bars (the music producers) are metal, on same principle as a tuning fork, which produce clear and most melodious notes, and never get out of tune; the bars are struck by strikers, the same as the wires are in a piano, only they work automatically instead of by the fingers. The strip of prepared paper in which the tune is stamped or perforated, is about 10 inches wide, and as it passes through the rollers and over the keys, the strikers spring through the perforations in the paper and strike the right note; this is all done automatically, without any assistance from the operator (except turning the rollers), and the tune is played perfectly. It would be one of the most appropriate presents to make any one, especially where there is no other musical instrument. Its execution is admirable, and its capacity or capability almost unlimited. It is selling faster than any musical instrument ever invented. The music is fine, and everybody delighted. The price of the Piano-ette is only **$5,** including a selection of popular tunes. Address, **The MASSACHUSETTS ORGAN CO. 57 Washington St., Boston, Mass., U. S. A., Sole Manufacturers.**

The "Autophone" pictured at the left was built by the same concern that manufactured the famous Ithaca Calendar Clocks in Ithaca, New York, from around 1880 to 1919. Thousands of these little devices were built, as were some larger models, by this concern. The fine print in the "Piano-ette" ad at the right is typical of the salesmanship of the day; to read it one would think the machine capable of reproducing the Boston Symphony Orchestra!

The largest disc machine marketed by Regina was not a music box at all, but was rather an orchestrion with the grandiose name of "Regina Automatic Concerto". This remarkable instrument played a piano, snare drum, a small bass drum, and a set of chimes. With a metal disc 32 inches in diameter, its dimensions are most impressive, and the opportunity to watch the intricate mechanism perform its task of switching discs is indeed a treat for the mechanically-inclined observer!

An interesting aspect of music discs and also of pinned cylinders is that the music arranger must always organize his material in such a way that a complete tune will result in just less than 360° of rotation. The ingenious ways they accomplished this necessarily were based on a partial rearrangement, or perhaps mutilation, of the composer's intent, and just as the mechanically inclined can have fun watching the machinery, the musically-inclined can enjoy these often-amusing distortions!

Many music boxes were built for public places, to be operated by insertion of a coin; the WurliTzer Company claims credit for having helped start this when at one time they were a large distributor for the Regina concern.

While not the same management, it is interesting to note that today's Regina vacuum cleaners have their historical roots in this famous company!

An interesting development of a device intended to be less expensive than the music box but still able to make music in the home is the so-called "roller organ." There were literally hundreds of different makes of these small table-top instruments built in both America and Europe during the late 1800's; some were operated by paper-roll music, others were by cheap pinned cylinders with headless nails being driven into wood in a pattern to produce the music much in the manner of a Swiss box.

For the most part, roller organs produced their sound from metal reeds, as does the harmonica or mouth organ. By turning a crank, the operator works a bellows through a crank mechanism; the air from the bellows passes to the proper reeds by note-holes in the paper tune-sheet, or in the case of the wood-cylinder organs, by valves tripped by the pins. One such machine, the Horton Autophone, was so simple it even did away with the crank and had the operator squeeze the bellows directly!

Manopan orgues à manivelle.

The Manopan was of European manufacture, and like its American counterparts, was typical of literally hundreds of different makes and models of this type of device. More elaborate ones were fitted with bells, drums, and other sounding devices to add a bit of "class" to the musical outpourings therefrom.

One may gain an idea of the tremendous market which existed for these little machines upon learning that for quite a number of years, the large mail order houses of Sears Roebuck and Montgomery Ward devoted entire pages of their catalogs to the products of the Autophone Company. The pinned cylinders were made in such enormous quantity that they were sold for as little as 18¢ each by these concerns!

Much of the music for roller organs was religious in character, which suggests that this type of music was prevalent in the homes of the late 1800's and early 1900's — this at a time when 'rag-time' was just starting to become popular, to the dismay of many mothers who feared for the evil influence of this development upon their children!

While the music box as collectors know it will never again be manufactured, it is interesting to note that children's toys modelled along the lines of the machines described here are frequently introduced to the market . . . so in a sense, the music box has never really left the American scene!

SATISFACTION GUARANTEED — MONTGOMERY WARD & CO.'S CATALOGUE No. 81 — SATISFACTION GUARANTEED

Roller Organs

The music is obtained from a roller furnished with pins similar to those used on a Swiss music box, which operate the valve keys, the latter being made of steel. The roller is made to revolve with gearing which also drives the bellows. The instruments are durable, all the working parts are easily accessible and are made of solid metal, the rollers and keys being mounted on castings. They are neatly finished and are genuine musical instruments which any child can play without teacher or practice. Regular full-sized organ reeds, 20 in number, are used, hence the quality of tone is similar to a reed organ, and the volume of sound will fill any ordinary sized hall. They will play hymns and popular airs with clearness and furnish acceptable music for any occasion. For dances, etc., they are admirable. We can furnish any kind of music, including Sacred, Spanish, Norwegian, German, popular airs and all the latest up-to-date selections. We quote a list of the best known and most desirable selections taken from the entire collection and a complete catalogue of music is sent with every organ. Every Roller Organ is shipped subject to 5 days' trial.

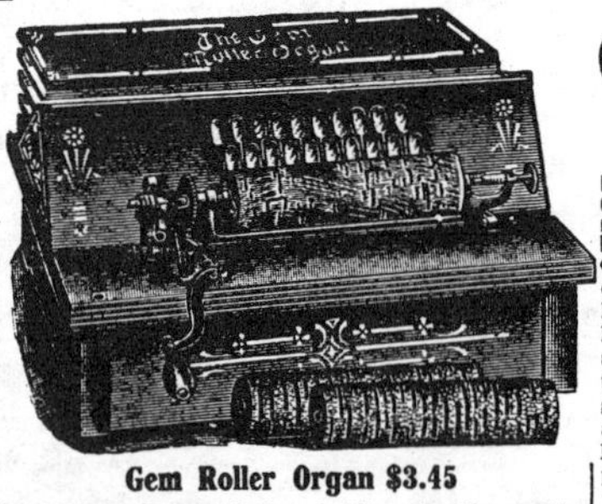

Gem Roller Organ $3.45

L 17996—Substantially built of thoroughly seasoned hardwood, neatly decorated, as shown in cut, and nicely finished. The dimensions are as follows: Length, 14½ in.; width, 12 in.; height, 8 in. It has twenty full size organ reeds, and 20 steel key valves. The roller is operated by turning the crank and the gearing of this style is on outside of case. Weight, boxed for shipping, 15 lbs. Price, including 3 rollers (your own selection) complete. Others ask $6.00. Each........................**$3.45**

Concert Roller Organ $7.60

L 17998—Much larger than the Gem and while it contains the same number of reeds and keys, has a larger bellows capacity, hence produces a greater volume of tone. The case is well made of hardwood, highly varnished and decorated. It has 20 full sized organ reeds, 20 steel valve keys and is played in the same manner as the Gem. The gearing is enclosed inside of case and protected by swinging door or lid, the latter being fitted with glass panel. This lid is also used as a "swell" by opening and closing at the proper time while playing. The dimensions of case are as follows: Length, 18 in.; depth, 15 in.; height, 12 in. The concert organ uses the same rollers as the Gem, complete list being given below. Shipping weight, 30 lbs. Price, including 5 rollers (your own selection). Others ask $12.00. Price **$7.60**

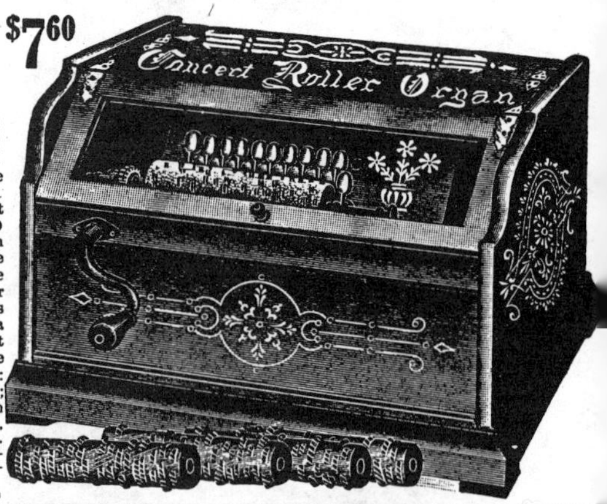

Records are not available to tell us how many of these little "roller" organs were built, but it must have been in the hundreds of thousands. These, too, were built by the Autophone Company of Ithaca, New York, which retailed them at about twice the prices given here. Both Sears, Roebuck and Montgomery Ward sold them, and with these low prices (The Gem was listed by Sears for as little as $3.25) they certainly must have moved huge quantities to justify the space in their catalogs year after year.

Reproducing Pianos -- The Artist In The Home

Unlike the roller organs and other small music machines built for the masses, the reproducing piano was a very expensive device, and consequently found its way only into the homes of the wealthy. With its capability of exact reproduction of the intonation, dynamics, and shading of the master artist who permitted his playing to be captured by the perforations in a paper music roll, it was truly the "high-fidelity" equipment of its day.

Without doubt the most spectacular development of the player piano was the mutation known as the "reproducing piano." These instruments are but little known today among the public at large, primarily because they were very expensive and when new could be owned only by wealthy persons, who were prone not to preserve them after they had tired of their musical output.

The player pianos discussed in Chapter 1 are capable basically of playing the notes of the music, but produce it in a mechanical-sounding fashion, with all notes struck with the same intensity — as if a robot were seated at the keyboard! It is true that with some practice and careful pedalling, a player pianist can impart a degree of expression to the music, but generally it is not the type of output that thrills the serious musician.

The reproducing piano, on the other hand, is a very sophisticated device capable of replaying music exactly as recorded by an artist, usually some renowned pianist — with the exact interpretation, the expression, the shading, the nuances, and the fire and gusto that he put into a personal playing of the work. Even unto this day, the capabilities of the reproducing pianos have never been equalled, even by the most sophisticated electronic high-fidelity sound equipment, for the reason that there can be no substitute for a real honest-to-goodness piano. A loudspeaker, however fine, simply is not the same as the actual instrument!

The history of the reproducing piano closely parallels the development of the ordinary foot-pumped variety. In 1904, the German firm of M. Welte & Sohne placed on the market their new development, the Welte-Mignon. The name derived from the fact that most of their production prior to this time had been large automatic instruments; pianos were small by comparison. This remarkable device stunned the musical world, as it became apparent that a real scientific "break-through" had been accomplished . . . the ability to have a mechanical piano repeat the exact performance of a living artist was as great an achievement to the technology of the day as was putting artificial satellites into space fifty years later!

Simply stated, what Edwin Welte and his brother-in-law, Karl Bockisch, had found a way to do was to capture an indication of the degree of force with which individual piano keys were struck by the artist as he played on a special piano rigged for this purpose, and to put this indication into the music roll in the form of extra perforations. The piano which played the rolls was equipped with apparatus which could "read" these extra holes in the paper, and translate them back into varying degrees of force with which its notes were played. This is not to suggest that there is anything simple about the actual apparatus — in fact, it is highly sophisticated in its concept, and must be carefully adjusted and regulated if it is to reperform a pianist's work accurately.

It's safe to say, though, that the results can be truly astounding to anyone who has never been privileged to hear a reproducing piano in fine condition. As ample evidence of this, one need only consider that every famous pianist who lived between the years 1904 and 1940 at one time or another made recordings of his work for reproduction on these instruments, and the advertising is replete with testimonial after testimonial from these artistic men and women. While it's probably safe to say that many of these rave notices were forthcoming for a fee, it's also safe to suggest that by and large, the artistic world of the day recognized the true worth of these remarkable machines and their ability to capture the personal interpretations of the great keyboard wizards of the day. Can anyone imagine

Mr. and Mrs. I. J. Paderewski listening to one of Mr. Paderewski's Duo-Art recordings

Practically every concert artist who lived during the first 30 years of the 20th century permitted his playing to be recorded for re-playing on the various makes of reproducing pianos. One of the most famous of these was Ignace Jan Paderewski, the Polish statesman-artist.

Recording a Selection

Cecile de Horvath recording for the Welte-Mignon (Licensee) in the Laboratory of the De Luxe Reproducing Roll Corporation

Hearing Her Record

Cecile de Horvath listening to her record on a Grand piano equipped with the Welte-Mignon (Licensee) in the Artists' room of the De Luxe Reproducing Roll Corporation

Various mechanical and electrical schemes were used to put artists' works on paper in the form of perforations. The makers of the Welte system claimed that theirs was the only one which would permit the artist to make a roll and then hear it played back immediately following the recording session. They made much of this fact in their advertising, implying that this feature somehow should result in more user satisfaction in the product.

great artists like Arthur Rubinstein or Josef Hofmann or Frank Milne prostituting their fine names on any device not fully worthy of their efforts?

The German-built Welte-Mignon was introduced to America around 1907, and as if the pianos themselves weren't expensive enough, the charges levied for the rolls were very high indeed. Three and four dollars per roll was common, and long numbers such as concertos which required two or three rolls to encompass their length often were sold for more like $15 — immense sums in their day, and quite beyond the reach of the ordinary man. But this freedom from competition was not to last for long.

The Aeolian Corporation, producer of the early Pianola reviewed in chapter 1, was hard at work during this period to come up with an effective device of their own to accomplish the reproduction of human playing. By 1913 they were able to put on the market their new machine, which they labelled the "Duo-Art" — presumably because of its capability of being played by hand as well as being able to perform on its own. This company controlled several makes of pianos, including the Stroud, the Steck, the Wheelock and the Weber in America, as well as other makes in Foreign lands, into which the Duo-Art mechanism was placed. In order to get their reproducing device in the instrument which even then was considered one of the truly great pianos, they entered into an arrangement with the Steinway organization, wherein Steinway built their pianos in such a way as to be able to receive the mechanism of the Duo-Art. These pianos were then sold to Aeolian, which in turn re-sold the machines through their own dealers. As a result of this relationship, the Steinway Company is the only American piano maker of consequence which never itself manufactured a player piano!

The Duo-Art was truly a remarkable device, when one considers that it was built for the next two decades with practically no change in its basic operating and controlling mechanism! Even today its adherents claim that it is the superior mechanism of those which made a dent in the reproducing market during the hey-day of these pianos.

The American Piano Company, another of the giant holding organizations in the music industry, naturally had to have a competing device, so in the middle 'teens they introduced their AMPICO — a reproducing device perfected by the mechanical wizard Charles Fuller Stoddard.

The Ampico operated on principles entirely different from that of either the Welte or the Duo-Art, but all were directed toward achieving the same end result. The Ampico was built into the Marshall and Wendell, the Fischer, the Chickering, the Knabe, and the Mason and Hamlin pianos in America — the latter being the finest of the line, representing effective competition for the Steinway reproducer controlled by Aeolian.

Just as strong in their beliefs that the Ampico system is superior, the enthusiasts for this method of reproduction are quick to deride the Duo-Art and the Welte! The fact is that when compared objectively, all three of these systems of operation produce remarkable results when properly adjusted and regulated in a fine instrument, and the arguments by the proponents of either of the methods are quite academic.

There were other systems on the market, too. The Angelus-Artrio, the Artecho, the Apollo, and the Celco, to name four — but only the "big three" achieved anything like real popularity in the marketplace.

In 1916 the Auto-Pneumatic Action Company of New York City entered into an arrangement with the German Welte firm under which their basic system of musical reproduction was made available, under license, for manufacture and distribution in the United States, as opposed to the prior importation of the European-made equipment. This device was known as the "Welte (Licensee)", and it was sold to independent piano manufacturers — some 112 makes in all. The music rolls were reduced in size from the European pattern to conform with the 11¼-inch width standardized in American practice in 1908, and certain modifications were made in the mechanism. This marketing scheme made it possible for those piano builders who were not in a position to develop their own reproducing devices to have an effective competitive item to offer the public, which might otherwise have selected primarily from the Duo-Art and Ampico offerings.

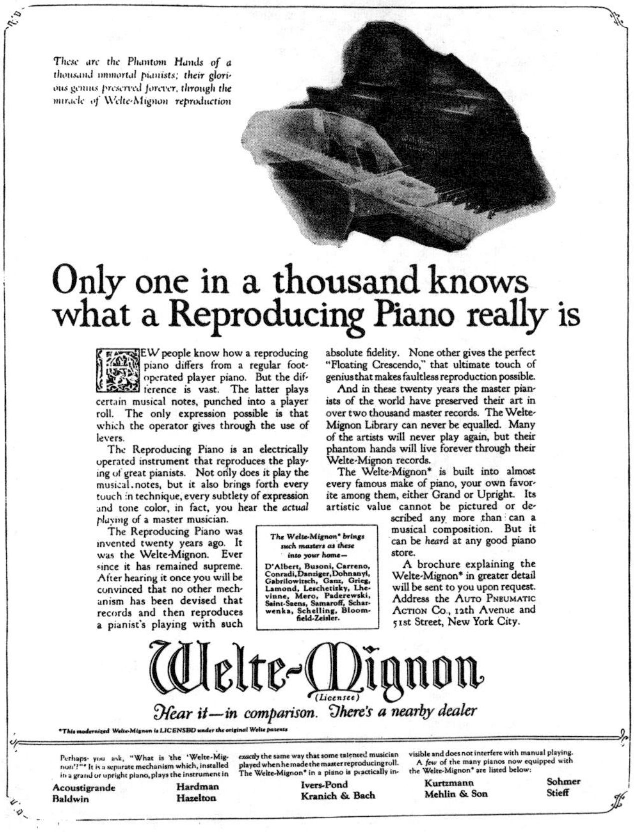

This advertisement tells a remarkable truth. A reproducing piano and an ordinary player piano are worlds apart in the characteristics of their musical output; the salesman of the day had to emphasize to their non-musically-inclined potential customers the importance of this difference in order that they would be willing to pay the considerably higher cost of the reproducing device.

THE AMPICO IN THE MUSIC ROOM OF VINCENT ASTOR, ESQ.

THE COMPLETE LEADERSHIP OF

The AMPICO

Certain products seem to gain most public favor through the snob appeal type of promotion. Expensive automobiles and reproducing pianos fit this bill very well.

Through this means, such magnificent instruments as the Baldwin, the Sohmer, the Bauer, and other pianos of artistic character were enabled to have reproducing capabilities and such machines are highly-desired collector's items today.

The music rolls for the Welte (Licensee) were available not only from the playing of the artists who were living after 1916, but re-cuts were made of those rolls recorded in Europe over a decade earlier. Thus it became possible to replay on American-made instruments the very earliest reproducing piano rolls made, by artists whose works otherwise would have faded into obscurity. Edward Grieg, for example — the great Norwegian composer of such masterpieces as his Concerto in A Minor — had several of his works captured forever in perforated-paper form by the Welte system; his death in 1907 precluded either the

The Stroud Duo-Art

While the reproducing piano is best known for its association with grand pianos, many of the mechanisms were placed in uprights as well. The Stroud was the least costly of the Aeolian Company's line, and consequently they are fairly common today.

The manufacturers of reproducing pianos and the rolls for them vied with each other to gain exclusive control of the work of various famous pianists. Historians agree that the Aeolian Company had the edge over the others in this respect; the outstanding public acclaim of the four great artists pictured in this advertisement is ample testimony of Aeolian's success in cornering a remarkable "stable" of the best pianists of the day.

Duo-Art or the Ampico from having original recordings by him. Thus any Welte piano-owner of today may have the privilege of having this great master's fingers play upon his very own instrument! Each make naturally vied to gain exclusive control of the performances of the best-known artists of the day.

Since each of the reproducing systems worked on a different basic principle in order to attain the same end result — the reproduction of actual hand-playing — it required that the music rolls for each system be different from the others. While the same physical dimensions as ordinary "88-note" piano rolls, the reproducing rolls are quite different in that they have in them the extra holes to re-interpret the music . . . and since the last rolls of this type were made in 1941 (Ampico), naturally they have become collector's items and values have risen in comparison to ordinary rolls.

Fortunately for those who treasure these instruments, as this book is written both Duo-Art and Ampico rolls are being recut. The choicest rolls from the thousands that were recorded during the period of popularity of these machines are now once again available to connoisseurs, thanks to the ingenuity and perseverance of expert technicians who have made a business of making these treasures once more available.

Two of the interesting marketing techniques employed in the promotion and sale of reproducing pianos were snob appeal and the demonstration concert. Because the mechanism of these instruments was highly sophisticated and costly, generally speaking only wealthy persons could afford them. This gave the promoters the opportunity to capitalize on the fact that to whatever rich person might be contemplating purchase, even richer ones were already so equipped! The picture of the Ampico in Vincent Astor's music room is typical of this type of merchandising effort, and it succeeded to a considerable degree. To this class of buyer, often the music itself was secondary, and the desire to "keep up with the Joneses" with what then proceeded to be nothing more than a fancy piece of furniture sold many expensive machines.

Of course when this happened the sale of rolls didn't benefit greatly, and the builders counted heavily on proceeds from them to make their money. Since only *their* rolls would fit their product, they had a captive market — something the builders of ordinary pump-pedal player pianos never had.

The demonstration concert was an ingenious way of showing to the public just what capabilities were inherent in the reproducing piano. The local dealer, or whoever was

When their advertisements weren't proclaiming that their make had the best artists performing exclusively, they were claiming that their make had the best capability of re-performing the work of the man who played for the roll in the first place. Even today authorities in the field haggle about which is best, particularly between the Duo-Art, the Ampico, and the Welte systems of operation.

promoting the instrument would arrange for a concert orchestra to be accompanied by a pianist, who would be performing on a seemingly-ordinary piano. The audience would be enjoying the strains of perhaps a Beethoven symphony, when all of a sudden the pianist would get up and walk away from his piano, leaving it to accompany the orchestra in a totally-unmanned mode of operation! The artist would have flicked the switch, leaving the startled patrons observing the reproducing piano at its best, playing in a human manner, without human control . . .

Such concerts were not just "stunts"; they were performed with famous orchestras all across the land. For example, the New York Times on November 18, 1917, in an article headlined "The Piano Played Itself", said this about Harold Bauer's "Duo-Art" Roll Interpreted With Orchestra:

"The Aeolian Company made a unique demonstration last evening in Aeolian Hall of their Duo-Art Piano, in which they had the assistance of the New York Symphony Orchestra, conducted by Mr. Walter Damrosch. The program contained orchestral pieces with a pianforte concerto, accompanied by the orchestra. Only, instead of a pianist, the concerto was played by the automatic action of the Duo-Art roll in a grand piano. It was a reproduction of Mr. Harold Bauer's interpretation of Saint Saen's G minor concerto. Mr. Bauer himself was in Chicago. Mr. Damrosch followed it as he would a player of flesh and blood, and created some amusement by his occasional close scrutiny of the moving keys of the keyboard and his success in "coming out even" with the roll, after the pianist had a pause which was filled in by the orchestra.

"The orchestra began with the overture to "Oberon", and after the concerto two of Mr. Percy Grainger's folk-song arrangements were played.

"There was a remarkable audience present in which musicians and pianoforte makers were conspicuous. The achievement of the Duo-Art roll and the orchestra together — an achievement which is perhaps unique — aroused great interest."

Eight months later, 5 June 1918, the Times reported a similar program in which the Ampico was featured in Carnegie Hall, accompanying works played by the Metropolitan Opera House orchestra — this time compositions by Beethoven, Liszt, and Rubinstein. The "artist" was Leo Ornstein, and the Times says that

"Mr. Ornstein at first sat quietly on the stage while, in popular phrase, "the piano played itself." Two motors, as the instrument's inventor explained, spurred a Knabe concert grand during the first movement of the concerto, reproducing in power and speed, in all dynamic gradation and tonal shading, the artist's interpretation. The sense of personality in touch and tempo was only visibly modified, a change in sight, not of hearing, when the power was switched off and Ornstein himself took the keyboard to finish the two remaining divisions of Rubenstein's concerto."

One of the most famous of these demonstrations was held in the Music Room of the New York Biltmore Hotel on October 8th, 1916. The New York Globe had this to say, under a title "Godowsky Versus Godowsky's Record":

"Once upon a time the great musician held that music could not exist where the artist himself did not actually produce the notes, and the player piano and phonograph called forth his silent scorn. So, also, not so long before that, the painter called the photograph humbug and the work of the devil, sir!

"The affair at the Biltmore held last Sunday would have been a scandal five years ago. For fancy, that great pianist Leopold Godowsky actually permitted a music roll record of his renditions to be heard on the Ampico immediately after he had performed them. And the audience compared notes!

"Indeed, as remarkable as the experiment itself is the extraordinary success achieved by the almost human instrument."

Because of the high cost of reproducing pianos, there was less justification for putting the mechanisms inside the cases of relatively inexpensive upright pianos as there was for their inclusion into grand pianos. While upright reproducing pianos were made in considerable quantity, the ones most desired by collectors today are the grands.

Another factor which undoubtedly influenced the high comparative numbers of grand pianos with reproducing mechanisms was that during the hey-day of these machines, there was also a great desire on the part of the average American home-maker to own a real grand piano. Space in homes was a smaller premium than it is today; during the Roaring 20's there was a lot of affluence (even though

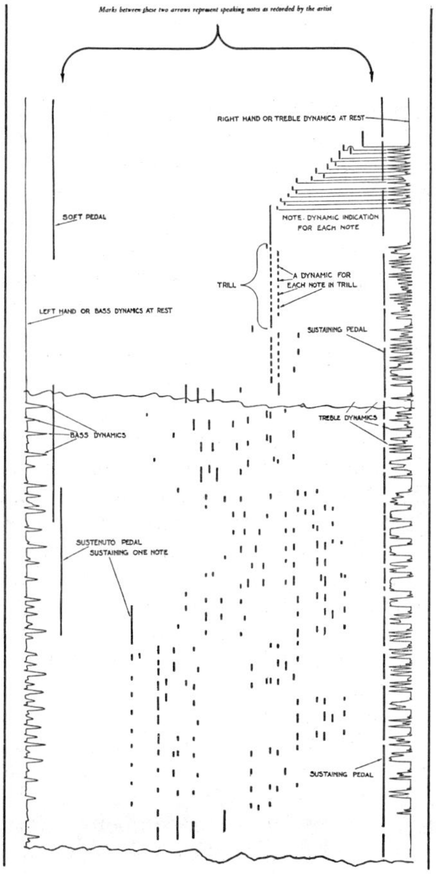

This photograph of a section from an original recording of Chopin's Etude in F Major shows how every detail of the artist's playing is graphically recorded while he plays. ¶With this absolutely authentic "tone picture" as a guide, the making of records for Welte Mignon (Licensee) Reproducing Pianos is free from every vestige of guesswork. Nothing is added or substracted that the artist does not himself put into his music, so that the record is not a mere approximation, but an exact reproduction of his playing. ¶What may be called the "film of the music camera" receives impressions of every detail of both his fingering and pedaling. ¶The exact position of every note played is fixed by faint vertical lines corresponding in number to the keys on the piano. The staggered lines on the extreme right and left are the means by which the mechanism, like the delicate needle of the seismograph that records the slightest tremor of the earth, graphically indicates exactly the degree of pressure with which the artist struck the keys, thus faithfully recording the finest shading of his interpretation.

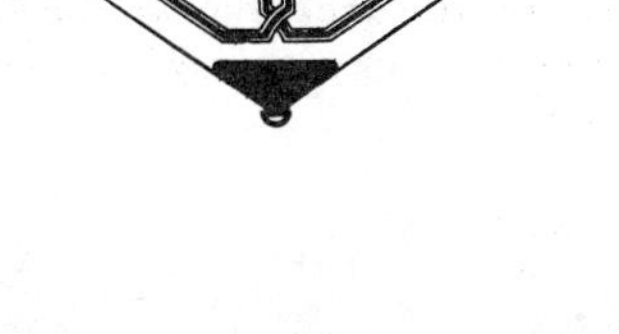

While this diagram reveals no trade secrets, it does give an insight in what is involved in the production of a music roll for a reproducing piano. There must be information in the form of punched holes to record not only the actual notes struck, but the degree of force with which they must be struck in order to re-perform the work. The devices which accomplish this are highly sophisticated examples of pneumatic engineering.

That reproducing pianos were once commonplace in wealthy homes is suggested by this sketch, wherein this Steinway seems to be ignored by all except one lady who passes a diffident glance. The Steinway Company enjoys the distinction of being the only American piano maker which never built a player piano of any type; those which had players in them were constructed especially for the Aeolian Corporation which installed the machinery and then re-sold the instruments. ***(picture courtesy of Henry Z. Steinway)***

a lot of it disappeared in 1929) and people wanted the best. The inevitable result was that while a lot of good pianos were built, there were a great many grands put on the market merely to meet price competition, which is another way of saying that a lot of second-rate instruments were unloaded on the public during this period.

Fortunately, most reproducing pianos brought enough of a price premium that these devices were generally found in the better grades of pianos.

The reproducing piano, like the ordinary player piano, was hailed as a great teaching device. But unlike the purely mechanical-sounding ordinary player, the reproducing piano could well be put to the test of comparing the works of the great artists for the benefit of serious students of music appreciation. The Welte advertisement on this page portrays graphically just how this was possible in terms of the speed of playing by different artists; the actual instrument had to be used for comparison of their pianistic techniques. Serious musicians have little difficulty in telling just who was responsible for the recording of the rolls which they hear, but not see, when played on a finely regulated reproducing instrument.

Widely-hailed (at least by its promoters) as an aid in teaching of the dance, a number of rolls were prepared which were designed to assist in learning everything from classical ballet to the Charleston. With these rolls were included little booklets which indicated the proper position of the feet and the various motions to which the body was to be put in order to perform the dance correctly. The ballet rolls are particularly fascinating; they show on them a sort of "body shorthand" which was developed to assist these students in performing the proper gyrations and movements as they carried out their exercises and contortions.

The reproducing capabilities of these pianos also laid rise to the "Accompaniment" rolls, which performed the piano portion of a duet with either voice or instrument such that the eager student could carry out his practicing without benefit of human partner.

The capabilities of the reproducing pianos were immense, and were not ignored by the sales executives of their manufacturers who must have stayed awake nights scheming new means for their promotion. Possibly more than in any other field of mechanical music the present and future generations owe them a debt of gratitude for their having seen to it that the artistry of every great pianist of that period was preserved for all time, not merely by capturing the sounds as does the phonograph, but by permitting continuing live performances on actual instruments in homes all across the land.

Not only can we today hear these performances, but we can make interesting comparisons of the ways in which popular music was styled to meet the public's fancy during the 35 year period in which these music rolls were marketed. What went over big in 1915 was strictly passe in 1930; the latest Ampico releases of the late 1940's offer highly sophisticated offerings in the popular vein.

Is it any wonder that reproducing pianos have become highly desired collector's items for music lovers everywhere?

~ ● ~

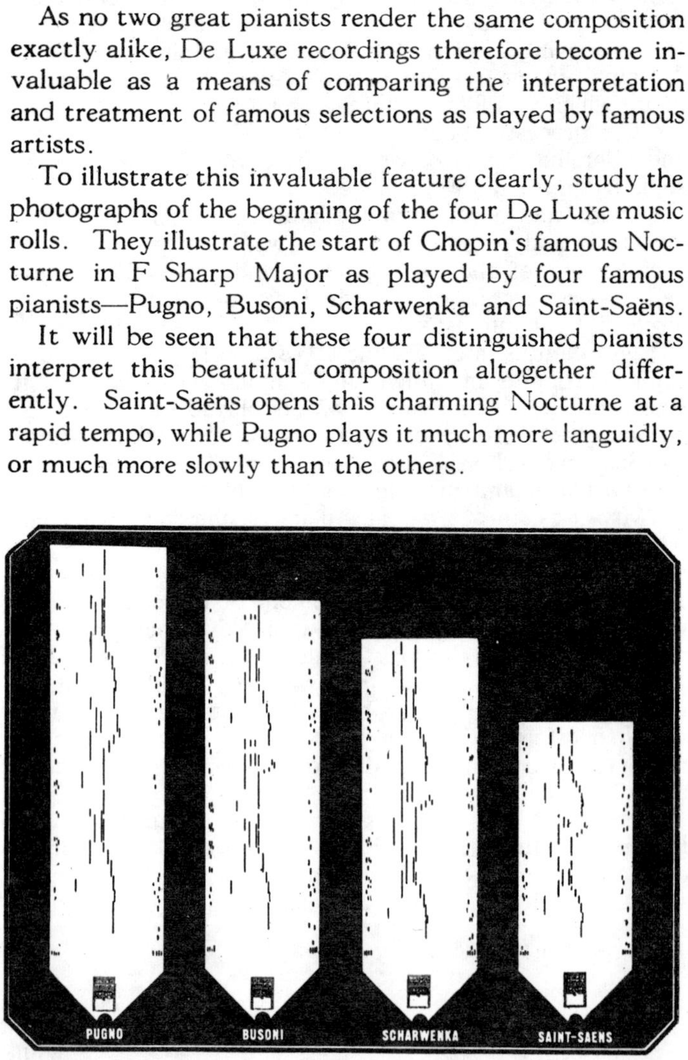

The makers of reproducing pianos made much of the potential of their instruments for the teaching of music appreciation. This advertisement tells how one may make comparison of the playing of various artists.

Automatic Music For The Millions

In Europe, Orchestrions (a term evidently derived from the concept of a mechanical orchestra) were devices of great musical capability, and were enormously expensive. They could be afforded only by very wealthy individuals and the royalty, although of course some were in public places for the enjoyment of the masses. The German Welte firm was one of the outstanding producers of these musical giants; they also originated the reproducing piano.

In a time when much of the industrial production of the World is devoted to the building of weapons of war and more and more diabolical ways to kill people, it's refreshing to think that in the days when automatic musical instruments were popular, the men responsible for their design and construction must simply have had a lot of fun in putting these things together!

Nowadays we hear the term "nickelodeon" applied to coin-operated pianos, but this term is historically incorrect, and it is quite incorrect to assume that the honky-tonky sounding devices foisted upon the American public are truly representative of the total picture of what was built for the enjoyment of all classes of people in the last half of the 19th Century and the first 30 years of the 20th.

The first automatic music-producing machines of a size greater than that of the table-top music boxes came from Germany in the middle part of the 1800's. Historians don't agree on just who got the movement started, but credit usually is given to Michael Welte, who concocted a huge machine which he called an "orchestrion", a term evidently inspired by the concept of a mechanical orchestra. This apparatus, almost 20 feet high and containing eleven hundred pipes together with an array of orchestra instruments, was an earnest attempt to simulate a human orchestra through the medium of music played from projecting pins on a wooden cylinder.

From this impressive beginning, the firm prospered and was able to peddle its wares all over the World. So realistic and inspiring was the music emanating from the cabinets of these monster machines that they found ready acceptance by wealthy individuals and members of the Royalty who were only too willing to part with huge sums equivalent to thousands of dollars for even the smallest models of these celebrated instruments.

The firm never hesitated to make known to the public those famous persons who had patronized them; the names cited on the accompanying advertisement are ones with which no critical buyer could possibly quarrel as to their impeccable taste in careful selection of the proper device for entertainment of their friends and guests! As we have seen, this "snob-appeal" was later applied with much success to the field of reproducing pianos.

Success always breeds imitation, and other companies were formed to grab their share of this lucrative market; some already in the business of making clocks and music boxes switched to this type of work. Names like Imhof and Mukle, Philipps, Frati, Dienst, Poppers, and Hupfeld made their mark on history as machines of these builders in Europe made their way into homes, castles, palaces, and

William Kramer's Sons' Atlantic Garden, Bowery, N. Y. City
Largest Orchestrion ever built, taking the grand prize at the Chicago World's Fair

This beautiful Welte orchestrion is said to have been destroyed in a fire many years ago. Alas, such was the fate of many of these magnificent machines. Their rarity today, as a result of this and other causes, makes them collector's items of a high order of desirability!

Brass Band Orchestrion
WOTAN

Replacing a military band of about twenty pieces.

Specifications

1st and 2d Cornet	Bourdon
1st and 2d Clarinet	Piccolo
Trumpet	Oboe
Alto	Flute with Xylophone
Trombone	Snare Drum
French Horn	Bass Drum
Baritone	(imitation Kettle Drum)
Bass	Cymbals and Triangle
Contra Bass	
Saxophone	

Dimensions

Height, 12 ft. 9 in. Width, 9 ft. 3 in. Depth, 4 ft. 10 in.

Case of dark gray-green oak with three illuminated glass scenes, the middle representing the fire scene from the Walküre picturing Siegfried and Brunnehilde. On each side panel are scenes from Switzerland, showing waterfalls. By means of special mechanism the water appears to be rushing continuously.

M·WELTE & SONS, INC·ORCHESTRIONS AND ORGANS

WELTE BRASS BAND ORCHESTRION "WOTAN"
replacing a brass band for band concerts in this park

Note proximity to the noisy roller coaster

It was common practice in Europe to assign names to various models of automatic instruments, much as today when automobiles are named after vicious creatures of the ocean or jungle. The Wotan was considered especially desirable where a great volume of sound was wanted, such as in amusement parks (next to noisy roller coasters!).

occasionally into a fancy beer-garden where the common man might be privileged to listen to the wonders of a completely automatic machine playing the works of the great composers.

These orchestrions were built not for purposes of attracting crowds, nor for bally-hoo reasons, but were rather for places of refinement and dignity. The attempt on the part of their designers was not to make noise, but to produce music of a character to satisfy the most fastidious of people and the most critical of musicians. More than one composer of renown wrote music for this type of instrument; no less a personage than Ludwig von Beethoven prepared his "Wellington's Victory" especially for playing on the Welte orchestrion! Modern classical musicians are prone to consider this a perfectly awful composition; when viewed in the light of the purpose for which it was intended originally it is cast into quite a different light indeed.

Unfortunately, most of these magnificent machines have not withstood the passage of time. When they became worn and in need of extensive repair, the persons who owned them often had tired of their music and were unwilling to make the necessary expenditures for their reconstruction. Since they were generally too large for storage in a back closet or a basement, they were broken up for scrap and burned as firewood . . . the magnificent Welte machine owned by Mme. Adelina Patti, the famous singer referred to at the top of the Welte advertisement, is a typical example of one which suffered this fate. Its last resting place was on the Island of Man, where it was burned during World War 2 for fuel. For reasons such as these, large orchestrions of European origin are seldom seen today; when they have survived, they are generally in private collections where they are considered rare treasures to be protected much in the manner of great art masterpieces.

Welte machines were imported to America by a branch of the firm located in New York City; European instruments of other makes found their way to the United States through distributors such as E. Boecker, also located in that city, and of course the greatest importer of all was the American firm of Rudolph WurliTzer.

The WurliTzer firm, founded in 1856 in Cincinnati Ohio by Rudolph WurliTzer who had arrived just a few years earlier on American shores from his native Germany, had made its mark on the musical instrument scene by importing directly from German builders, and then selling to the public without dealing through distributors and other intermediaries. By aggressive merchandising and advertising the firm had achieved a place of real prominence by the late 1800s, and was a major factor in the distribution of all types of instruments from violins to merry-go-round organs.

It was the latter device that got WurliTzer into the piano and orchestrion business. A builder of merry-go-round organs in North Tonawanda, New York by the name of Eugene DeKleist ventured to the Cincinnati offices of the firm to interest them in the organs he was building. The visit resulted in his building for WurliTzer, under contract, a new automatic piano which could be operated upon insertion of a coin.

The WurliTzers — father and three sons — had a decade or so earlier been very successful in marketing the products of the Regina Company that we have seen in the chapter on music boxes, but their interests were in making the machines operable by coins, where the general public could easily play them in stores, saloons, and other places of assembly. It appeared to the WurliTzers that there was a tremendous potential market in a coin-operated player piano, for only then was the public beginning to become aware of the fascination of these marvelous devices. It was apparent to them, and to other marketers as well, that while there were millions of Americans who would like to hear the music produced by these new automatic marvels,

THE RUDOLPH WURLITZER CO.

Gentlemen:

Our Style 17, Wurlitzer PianOrchestra has been playing continuously about twelve hours every day for the past nine months and it as good today as when you first installed it. Repairs have been practically nothing, even the piano has not required tuning.

This instrument has increased our business fully 40 per cent. We have a great many business people in our vicinity who come in purposely to hear it play. If same could not be replaced I would not part with it for many times the amount I paid for it.

Very truly yours,

L. RAPHAEL, Prop.

THIS HANDSOME THEATRE, AT PITTSBURG, PA., USES A WURLITZER PIANORCHESTRA AS A MUSICAL ATTRACTION.

The term "nickelodeon" is a later-day adaptation of the word originally used to describe a theatre to which the admission was five cents. The Bijou Dream of Pittsburg is a classic example of the type of edifice from which the term originated.

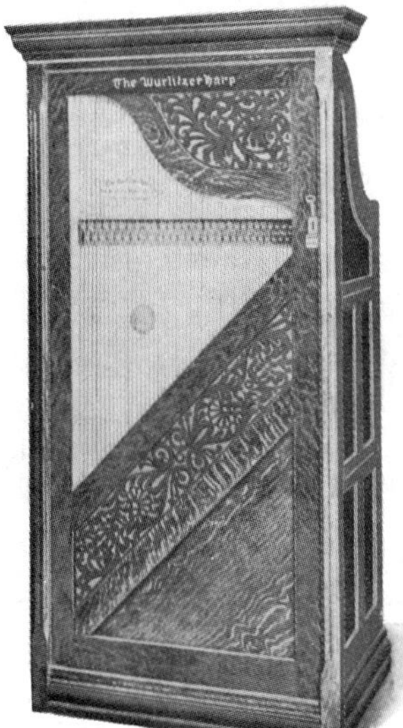

Three early instruments. The WurliTzer Tonophone in the center picture, shown yielding a bonanza of nickels to the proprietor of a turn-of-the-century whiskey emporium, was the first in that company's line of distinguished automatic pianos. The WurliTzer Automatic Harp at the left was made under contract by a firm in Rising Sun, Indiana; of the almost 1500 originally built, only a handful remain today as choice collector's items. The WurliTzer Pianino at the right was built in a variety of models for almost 30 years, establishing a record for continuous production of a basic instrument.

there were a large proportion who could ill-afford to put forward the amount of money required to own one — and who therefore would be eager to drop nickels into slots to satisfy their musical hunger.

WurliTzer's first attempt to capture this market was the DeKleist Tonophone, a bulky piano played from a large wooden cylinder. It was an immediate success, and the resulting business to the firm of DeKleist which built them under contract was to make the owner a wealthy man. The entire activity was so profitable for the WurliTzer company that they decided to take over the operation themselves, so they purchased the control of the DeKleist organization, whereupon the original owner went into politics for a while and then retired to a life of leisure on his profits from the WurliTzer transaction.

Having thus established themselves in the manufacturing business in North Tonawanda, New York, the Rudolph WurliTzer Company then proceeded to delve into other markets, and this plant eventually became World-famous for its production of huge pipe organs used in the giant movie palaces of the 1920's. . . these became known as the "Mightly WurliTzers", and are considered today as truly the 'king of instruments' by most connoisseurs of the musical scene. (while not the subject of this book, it is interesting to note that it was written into the purchase contract of each WurliTzer pipe organ for theatre use that the description "Pipe Organ" was never to be used on the marquee of the building in which it was installed. The terminology always to be used was *"The WurliTzer"!*)

While WurliTzer was already a giant in the industry, other concerns were eager to exploit the eagerness of the citizens to hear automatically-played music in public places. Notable among early pioneers was the National Electric Piano Company located in St. Johnsville, New York, and to it goes the credit for having first placed a paper-roll-played coin-operated piano — the Peerless —

Cincinnati showroom of the Rudolph Wurlitzer Company in 1906. A large array of orchestrions, coin-operated pianos, band organs and other automatic musical instruments greeted the would-be buyer.

on the musical scene in the United States. This company produced a great variety of models during the next two decades, many of which were what may be termed the *American variety* of "orchestrion" — a player piano, coin-operated, to which various embellishments in the form of drums, traps, pipes, xylophones were added to lend variety and interest to the music. Other concerns will be seen later.

As is wont to happen, the firm producing the Peerless passed to heirs who were less interested in keeping the business together than they were in other things, and it is said that the entire enterprise was lost in a gambling party!

In the meanwhile, WurliTzer had decided to import to America the giant musical machines built by the German firm of Philipps and Sohne, and an array of these are shown in the 1906 picture of the Cincinnati showrooms of this concern. Alas, these large instruments eventually suffered the same types of fate as others of their dimensions, and very few indeed are left to entertain those of later generations. It is some consolation to know that only their rarity makes them valuable, but collectors who appreciate these finer things in life would always be happier if more of them were still here to take their places aside the numerous instruments which have survived the junkman's axe.

North Tonawanda, New York, was the home of several firms engaged in mechanical music activity, much of which was related to the building of merry-go-rounds centered in that upstate community. The story of the production of these amusement devices would fill a book; suffice to state that each needed an automatic organ which would keep proper tempo with the whirling and the ups-and-down of the elaborately carved horses and other animals as they went on their merry circular path.

These needs were first met by the DeKleist Company, whose founder had learned the trade of constructing automatic merry-go-round organs — more familiarly called "band organs" — in Europe. Three other concerns, in addition to WurliTzer which absorbed the DeKleist firm, ap-

The scene below greeted visitors at the Louisiana Purchase Exposition in St. Louis in 1904. The instruments here depicted were manufactured under contract to WurliTzer by the DeKleist Musical Instrument Manufacturing Company of North Tonawanda, New York, with WurliTzer being the sales agent. Shortly thereafter the latter firm assumed control of the whole activity, and the DeKleist name was dropped. Eugene DeKleist became a wealthy man through this association, and the name WurliTzer became known far and wide through the famous instruments which were built in their North Tonawanda factories — not the least of which were the "Mighty WurliTzer" pipe organs used in the movie palaces of the 1920's.

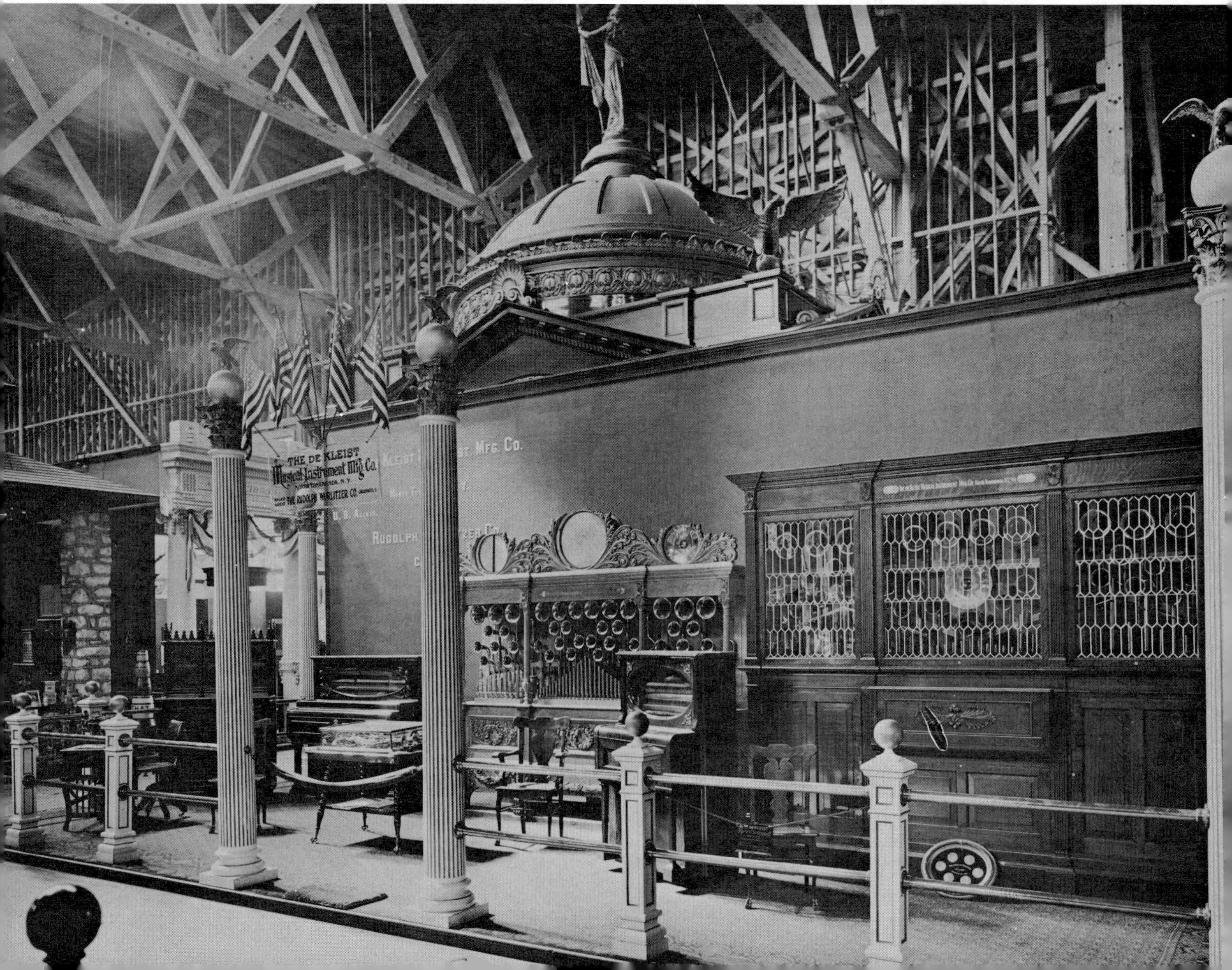

Early band organ manufacture in America centered in North Tonawanda, New York. This brass horn model 192, put out by the North Tonawanda Musical Instrument Works, appeared about 1910. It is said that this company was started by a group of disgruntled WurliTzer employees. It eventually was purchased by the Rand Visible Records Company, a forerunner of today's Sperry-Rand Corporation. Can it therefore be said that this band organ is an ancestor of the Univac?

peared on the scene during the first 25 years of the 20th century. One was the North Tonawanda Musical Instrument Works, which is said to have been started by a group of disgruntled WurliTzer employees, and it not only built a fine line of these machines, but it also imported European machines for distribution under its own name.

This company also built a variety of coin-operated pianos and orchestrions, and also some movie-theatre pit instruments. The concern was purchased in 1917 by the

Band organs are best known in America for their service on merry-go-rounds, which were also made in quantity in North Tonawanda, N.Y. This picture shows the arrangement by which the WurliTzer model 146 was powered from the same machinery which spun the patrons of these amusement devices on their merry way! The model 146 was undoubtedly one of the most popular built by WurliTzer; its retail price was under $1100.

Rand Visible Records Company, which did so in order to acquire the cabinet-building facilities for their line of office furniture and equipment. The officials of Rand had little or no interest in the building of the automatic pianos and organs, but nevertheless continued them for several years thereafter. Since this company was an ancestor of today's Sperry-Rand Corporation, builders of giant computers, afficianados of the antecedent instruments are quick to point out that they must truly be the forerunners of today's automatic brains. This is surely stretching a point, but there does seem to be some sort of relationship between the concept of storing electronic information in magnetic memory circuits and storing music in pieces of perforated paper!

Another firm was known by the name of Artizan, and the history of the formation of this concern is not clear, nor is the relationship — if any — between this one and the one previously mentioned. Its band organs incorporated

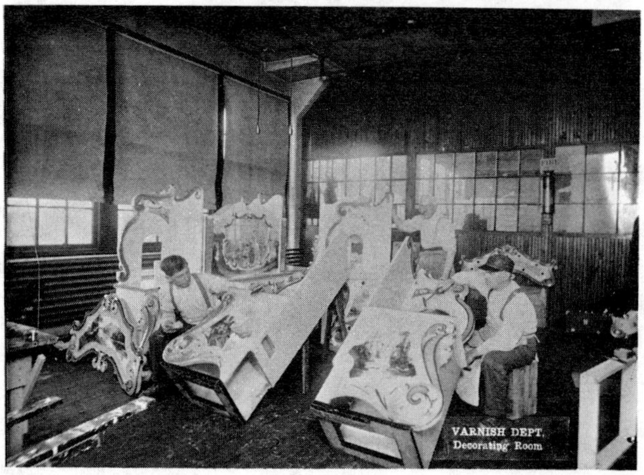

The two scenes above are from the archives of the WurliTzer Company, and show a real assembly-line type of operation in the production of these noisy, but much-loved instruments of a former day.

many technical improvements over previously-known concepts, such that they are considered especially desirable by today's collectors.

The third was the Niagara Musical Instrument Manufacturing Company, which put out a rather complete line of both band organs and automatic pianos. All the North Tonawanda-made instruments seem to have certain family resemblances; there is little doubt but that some technical information must have flowed between the firms.

One point is quite clear when it comes to American-made band organs: they were built not for the production of music as such, but their output was intended to be to attract crowds, to make ballyhoo for carnival purposes, and just generally to be loud and raucous. While connoisseurs of the American band organ who thrill to their particular type of musical output may protest this thought, it is pretty difficult to argue that music from them can in any way be compared with the thrilling output of the European fair organs.

For purposes of this book, European automatic organs may be considered in three general groups: *Fair organs, Street Organs,* and *Dance Hall organs*. All of these operate on the same general principle; they all have bellows which are actuated to produce pressure to blow through pipes to make the music, most have other bellows which make vacuum to operate the valves to control the pipes, and they usually play from perforated music. Unlike the typical American organ, however, the music is not perforated into rolls of paper, but it is put into sheets of heavy cardboard which are hinged together into one long continuous strip, or "book".

The differences in the machines are mainly in the types of tones produced by the pipes, resulting from differing methods of "voicing", in exactly the same manner as the various ranks of pipes in a church or theatre organ are regulated and fixed so that they present a differing variety of "voices" when mingled together or played separately.

The fair organs were built primarily for the use in traveling fairs, which would in America be called carnivals. These instruments were made by a number of firms; perhaps the one known most prominently is that of Gavioli et Cie of Paris. The picture below is of an immense machine of their make, and it is readily apparent that anything of this character is truly a work of art! The elaborate facades of all European automatic organs are a joy to behold, and the wood-carving upon them is essentially a lost craft. It is hard to believe that at one time many men spent their lives in the artistic decoration of the thousands of such devices that were built for the enjoyment of fair-goers everywhere on the European continent.

It is quite impossible for a written description such as this to give any concept of the beauty of the music forthcoming from a machine of this character. With rank upon rank of pipes of different tonal output being combined in various harmonies throughout the playing of a composition, together with appropriately-scored accompaniment of drums, bells, and other traps, there is simply nothing else in the musical world which can remotely compare with these fair organs. As in the case of any automatic instrument, the musical results obtained are in direct proportion to the character of the arrangements cut into the perforated paper or cardboard, and a large instrument with many ranks of pipes and numerous registers provides unlimited possibilities for clever application by the talented persons who do this work.

Street organs are an adaptation of the fair organ, and are today found in Holland where they are used to beg money from persons on the streets much as organ-grinders

The European fair organ at its greatest! Built in 1909 by the Paris-based firm of Gavioli, this fantastic instrument was restored by George Parmley of Durham, England, and it is possibly the largest organ of its type ever built in terms of its musical capabilities. It is mounted on a trailer. *(Fair Organ Preservation Society photo)*

Beautiful organs such as this one are still found on the streets of Holland, where they delight not only the tourists, but the natives of that country who consider them a prize national asset. Unlike the typical American band organ whose outpourings are of a "ballyhoo" nature, the European instruments have magnificent musical qualities. This instrument is known as "The Flower Girl"; it is common practice for these machines to have such names, as each is unique not only in appearance but musical character.

and their monkeys used to do in many places. The Dutch street organs provide a type of music which is heard nowhere else in the World, and today they are considered national treasures not only by the afficianados of this type of thing, but by the Dutch people generally who have come in recent years to realize that they are a marvelous attraction for tourists!

The pattern of operation of these is rather interesting. Generally they are owned by individuals who rent them to two qualified persons — one of whom turns the giant wheel to operate the instrument, and the other who begs for money from the passers-by. Because this type of activity can easily degenerate into a nuisance, at one time organs were practically banned from the streets of such famous old cities as Amsterdam, the Hague, and Rotterdam.

This Hooghuys organ stands in the private collection of Mr. W. J. Barlow of Cleobury Mortimer, England, where it has delighted visitors from many lands. *(Photograph by Mr. Fred Guy)*

Dutch children stand enthralled before one of the wonderful organs which are heard in their country. This picture is from the book *"FROM MUSIC BOXES TO STREET ORGANS"*, published by the Vestal Press and devoted entirely to the history and characteristics of these interesting instruments. The organs are played by one man who turns a large wheel, while his partner begs money from persons passing by. When revenues drop, they push it on to some more promising location.

However, in recent years the Dutch have come to the realization that there is much to be gained from promotion of their street organs rather than the banning of them, so now those who operate them are licensed by the city police, who insure that the privilege of their operation on the city street is not abused. The operators and owners are required to have their instruments in good working order and in proper tune, and other regulations are applied pertaining to how many may be on the streets and where they may be located. The result of this control is that a real treat is in store for any person who has the privilege of hearing one of these fine machines on the streets! Of course the instruments are always operated by hand, and are always pushed through the streets by hand as well.

Periodically contests are held between owners of the organs, where judges preside to make rulings on the quality of the musical arrangements used and the performance of the instruments, and these affairs are the subject of much National interest and encouragement. Fortunately, at least for the Dutch, recognition of the worth of these machines is now such that vigorous efforts are made by many interested parties to prevent their purchase and exportation to other countries. Tourists to Holland are thus assured of much fine musical entertainment in future years as they walk the streets of the cities of that fine land.

Dance hall organs are now found mainly in Belgium, where some 600 still are used to entertain patrons of beer gardens and dance halls. The Belgian people seem to have a national characteristic of enjoyment in patronizing fine establishments where they may take the entire family, drink a little beer, dance a while, exchange greetings with their friends, and generally have a good time to the tune

Many European mechanical organs are literally as large as small buildings! This Belgian Mortier dance-hall organ evidently was temporarily set up outdoors for picture taking; its styling would suggest that it was built during the 1930's. The visitor to Belgium today can hear many of these machines, as several hundred are still on location in dance halls and beer gardens throughout the country, and in fact small numbers of them are still being manufactured.

of very large automatic instruments. Most such halls are open on a 24-hour basis, and the organs play almost continually — including many popular American tunes of the 1920's!

Mortier of Antwerp was one of the most prominent builders of these organs, but today the one firm which still manufactures them — as many as 5 or 6 each year — is Decap of that same city. The most recent productions are based around electronic organs, enhanced by ranks of pipes, drums and traps, xylophones and glockenspiels, all played from perforated cardboard music books. While very few new instruments are being built, there are several individuals in the Low Countries who make their living by preparing music for use in them. Visitors to Belgian dance halls may be assured of hearing a goodly share of the latest musical hits of the day!

One of the most fascinating, and one of the least-known of the automatic instruments is the silent-movie pit photoplayer. Between 1910, when movies started to amount to something and were shown in what were called "nickelodeons" (odeon is the Greek for theatre; the term therefore suggests a theatre which could be attended for five cents), and the late 1920's when "talkies" came into being, there was always a need for some type of musical accompaniment to silent films.

The earliest nickelodeons depended on a piano player to furnish the musical dialogue, and he (or she) would do his best to play music suited to the demands of the film on the silver screen above as it changed scenes and moods. As theatres grew in size to meet public demand, large pipe organs were built and installed to provide the musical portion of the shows, and they were veritable one-man-operated orchestras when operated by a clever organist.

But there were plenty of theatres across the land which were too small to justify large organs, yet needed something more than merely a piano. This fact, combined with the ever present need to keep the salary of the operator as low as possible, made a market for glorified player pianos called "photo players" which were specially constructed to meet the needs of the silent movie houses.

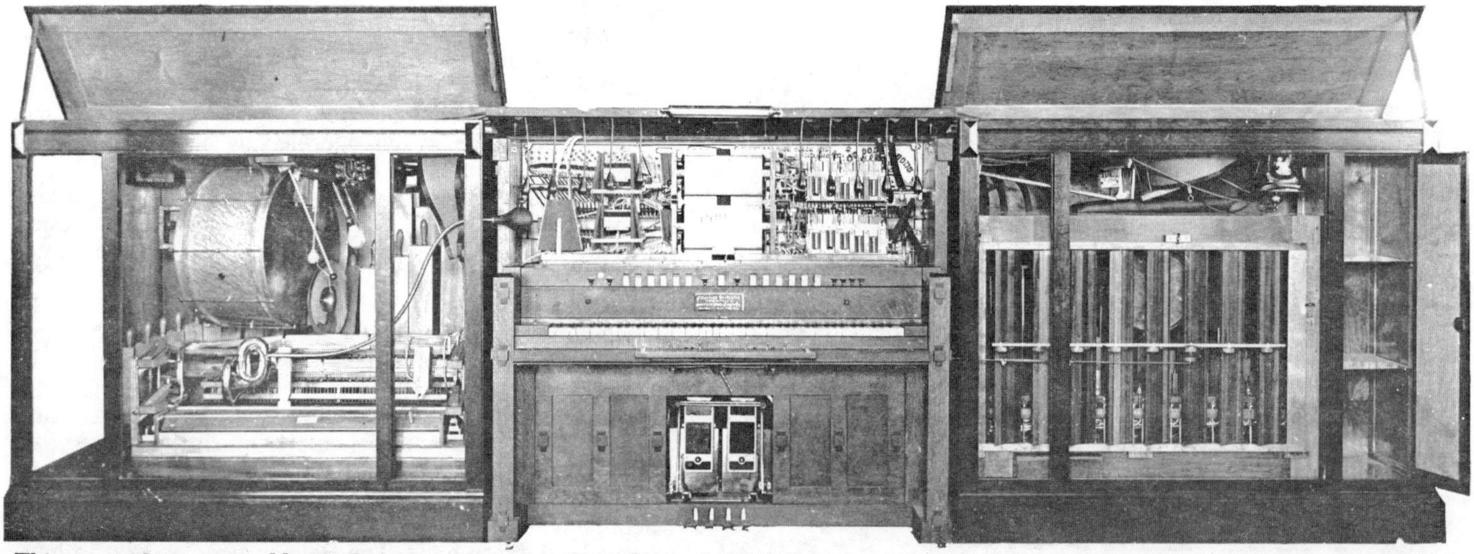

This magnificent assemblage of noise makers is a Fotoplayer, built for use in the orchestra pits of silent movie houses before the days of "talkies". The operator worked the player piano in the center, and pulled cords to create sound effects such as train whistles, fog horns, wind, pistol cracks, crockery smashes, antelope bleats or what-have-you, to be added to the sonorous outpourings of various ranks of organ pipes located in the two side-chests. The picture directly above shows one of these fantastic music machines of a by-gone day in its theatre location.

Many firms built theatre-pit photoplayers; this one was by WurliTzer.

A busy scene in the music-roll perforating room at the WurliTzer factory. The hey-day of the mechanical piano coincided with that of the silent movie, and business establishments such as this one had plenty of work to do to meet the insatiable demands of the public for the latest hits of the day on their favorite instruments, whether located at the local pool-hall or in the neighborhood 'nickelodeon' theatre.

They were built by several concerns, but generally all took the form of a basic player piano (usually electrically operated) to which large chests full of organ pipes and sound effects were fitted on either side. In most cases provision was made for two music rolls, so that the operator could place different types of "mood music" on the instrument thus permitting instant changes from "chase" scenes to "light dramatic", or perhaps from "struggle" to "mysterioso", as required by whatever was happening on the screen at the particular moment.

Various schemes were used to provide the sound effects; WurliTzer machines provided a row of toe-buttons to actuate the horses hooves, the doorbells, the fire gong or whatever the picture demanded; the American Fotoplayer provided a series of leather cords which the operator pulled as he saw fit to meet the appropriateness of the scene. But whatever method was used required some degree of skill on the part of the person operating the apparatus, whether he be a qualified pianist or merely some teen-ager hired to switch rolls occasionally, if the music was to be of any degree of desirability.

It's safe to assume, however, that all too frequently the manager merely started the machine in the morning and let it clang on all day long and halfway through the night on the theory that most of his patrons wouldn't know the difference anyway in musical moods and there was little point in spending good money to hire a trained musician for his class of clientele!

Sincere efforts were made to provide properly trained personnel by some distributors, however, and a good example is the famous old firm of Lyon and Healy in Chicago. This company operated a school to train qualified operators for the American Fotoplayer, for which they had the sales agency, although they were careful to make certain that their trainees read a large sign at the entrance to the practice rooms which stated "NOTICE! We do not guarantee to furnish positions to Fotoplayer students."

While most instruments of this type had sound effects, at least one popular model, the Reproduco, contained only pipes to accompany the piano. Suitable for houses of from 250 to 400 seats, this dandy little machine found great favor among movie house managers, and it served double-duty for the manufacturers, for it was also sold widely to mortuaries and funeral homes, thus greatly increasing its marketability.

It's sad, but true, that photoplayers of any type are extremely scarce today. When their usefulness was over at the advent of "talkies" there was little reason for them to be retained by their owners, and what with the hard use most of them got — hammering away day and night 7 days each week in most cases — most were probably ready for for the junkman, anyway!

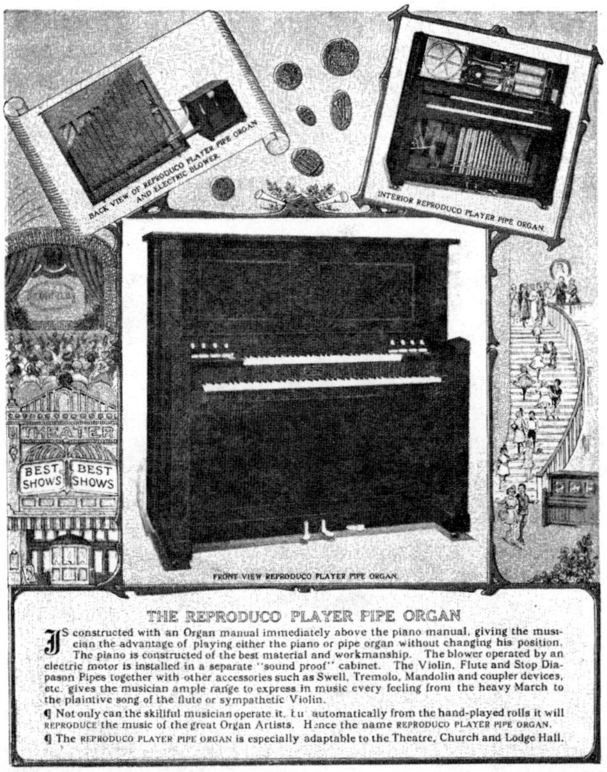

This combination piano and pipe organ was a great favorite for the smaller theatres of two or three hundred seats. Player roll music for these and other photoplayers had several general classifications — Hurry, Mysterioso, Chase, Indian, Oriental, Struggle, Comedy, Snappy, Light Dramatic, Heavy Dramatic, and so forth — such that the non-musically-trained operator was at least in theory always able to match the mood of the music to the scenes cast upon the silver screen, merely by checking the label on the box!

This piano contained a set of flute pipes to accompany the renderings of the keyboard. The line was manufactured by the Marquette Piano Company of Chicago, which apparently felt that in using the name "Cremona" the public would somehow establish a relationship with the musical excellence of the celebrated violin-maker Antonio Stradivarius, whose home was Cremona, Italy.

For "ricky-ticky" music, nothing has ever approached the coin operated piano. As indicated earlier, these first appeared on the American market around 1900, and it wasn't long before there was plenty of competition in the field for the nickels of the patrons of those public places which saw fit to capitalize on the newly-found desire of everyone to hear automatic music. Coin-operated pianos were literally everywhere — in stores, saloons, bawdy-houses, railroad stations, pool parlors, lodge halls — you name it; they had 'em!

Most were played for a nickel, but occasionally they were built to command a higher premium. At least one firm, and probably the others too, built some with *fifty-cent* slots for particularly high-toned houses of ill repute, where undoubtedly they were fitted with snappy two-minute tunes to stimulate a fast turnover of trade!

While Boston, Massachusetts, and New York City had been the early centers of piano manufacture in the United States, as the population expanded westward the great railroad center of Chicago became the hub of this activity. This was a well-established fact by the time that coin-pianos became really popular, with the result that great numbers were built there. Seeburg, Marquette, Coinola, Western Electric and Mills are famous names associated with this community, and there were many lesser-known ones which originated there, too.

No doubt the best-known Chicago name today is Seeburg, for it is one of the very few that survived the 1929 crash and subsequent depression to continue in other fields — notably with the coin-operated phonograph.

Justus P. Seeburg was a Swedish immigrant, who had learned the trade of piano-making in his native country. Arriving in America in the late 1800's, he was quick to perceive the possibilities inherent in the coin-operated piano, and it wasn't long after the turn of the century that he had established the J. P. Seeburg Piano Company which devoted itself only to the production of these automatic instruments. A good product combined with aggressive merchandising made this company a front-runner in the field, and among the surviving instruments today, there are probably more Seeburgs than any other.

The Cremona piano, built by Chicago's Marquette Piano Company, was very popular, and best-known for its quality features. While it's not clear how beautiful bird's-eye maple veneer on the inside of the cases made the pianos any better, this was typical of the type of workmanship that went into these particular instruments . . . as was the use of "new-born calfskin" in the pumps in the place of the usual cowhide or lesser material. Whatever the reason, they built beautiful instruments, and today's connoisseurs of the field are in general agreement that the Cremona is undoubtedly the "Rolls-Royce" among coin pianos.

$1,200

STYLE F

Case Design Patented

INSTRUMENTATION:

PIANO, VIOLIN AND MANDOLIN, OR PIANO, FLUTE AND MANDOLIN

Massive appearing artistically designed case, 6 inches higher than an ordinary piano, but no larger in the length or width. Featuring a row of small art glass panels at top and elaborate coppered art glass illuminated panels and colonial art lamps hanging at sides. Double veneered hardwood case finished in mission oak. Equipped with automatic mandolin and pipe attachments, loud and soft lever, and tempo regulator on outside below key-bed. Any instrument can be shut off at will. Magazine slot registering 1 to 20 coins. Music roll "S" contains from 10 to 20 selections on Seeburg rewind system. Art glass design subject to change without notice. When ordering specify whether violin or flute pipes are desired. Height—5 feet 6 inches. Width—2 feet 4 inches. Length—5 feet 4 inches. Weight boxed for shipment about 1050 pounds.

The beauty of Seeburg Automatic Instruments lends distinction to any surroundings in which they are placed.

Then, as today, manufacturers dare not stray too far from the product styling generally accepted by the public at a particular period in time. Note the similarities of this Seeburg Style F and the Cremona Flute Piano Style G, shown elsewhere on this page.

The Cremona Three in One—Electric Piano, Player-Piano and Regular Piano. Easily Convertible at Will.

Cremona No. 3
With lower panel removed, showing perfect accessibility of motor and mechanism, and easy, instantaneous insertion of music rolls.

"Easy, instantaneous insertion of the music rolls" may have been overstating the case in this Cremona ad, but compared with the LINK piano on the next page there is merit in this point. Plain glass fronts were as popular as were art glass styles; this instrument featured beautiful bevelled panes with singing canaries painted in the center of each section.

COINOLA CABINET PLAYER

The Coinola Cabinet player borrowed an idea from the old "push-up" style of device, and permitted one to make a coin-operated instrument from an ordinary piano in a matter of minutes.

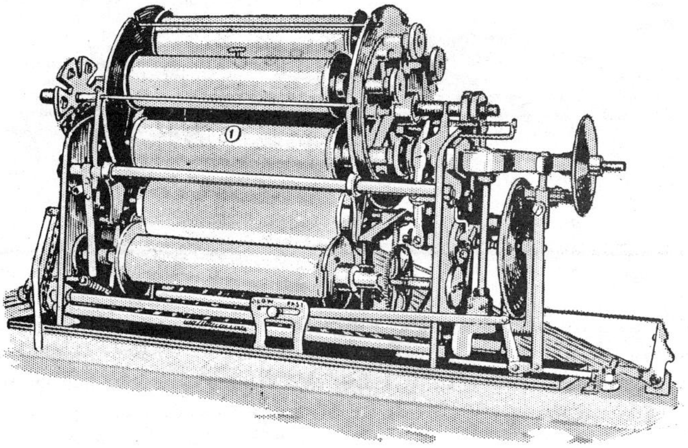

WurliTzer

One of the most complicated devices ever put into any automatic instrument was the WurliTzer automatic music roll changer. With this device it was possible to have 30 tunes played without repeating, as it held six rolls of five tunes each. Each roll plays through entirely, then rewinds; the entire magazine rotates 60°, and the next roll is started. At 5¢ per tune, this was $1.50 added to the till of the proprietor of the piano — not an insignificant amount in its day.

STYLE "K"—"Midget Orchestrion"
Case design patented
Piano, mandolin and xylophone.

Style "L"—Smallest Electric Piano made. Also has Mandolin Attachment. Uses Standard 65-Note Music Roll. Dimensions—Height: 51½"; Width: 36½"; Depth: 23½"

Two of the most popular coin operated pianos ever built were the Seeburg Style L at right and the Style K at the left. Available also with trapwork for additional embellishment of the music, the K then became the Style KT. Its art-glass Eagle, found in most surviving examples, makes it known among collectors as the "Seeburg Eagle" model.

In spite of whatever features the others might have boasted, however, today's collectors also are in general agreement that the most highly-prized machines to be had are those made by the Operators' Piano Company under the Coinola name. This is not because of any special mechanical gimmickry, but because the paper rolls used with all but the plainest models were of outstanding quality in terms of the music arrangements scored for their use. These rolls — the type "O" — had narrower perforations than those used by other makes — and it was possible therefore to get more musical possibilities per foot of paper.

The arrangers who scored these rolls made effective use of this feature, with the result that there is really nothing that can compare with good "0" roll music for those who enjoy the real "ricky-ticky" type of output. For some reason not clear, the Operators' Piano Company never capitalized on this in their advertising, and it seems that they missed a good bet by not so doing.

One famous name in automatic pianos survived in a

A Magnet for—

Style 2 -- B

Piano, Mandolin, Snare Drum, Triangle, Tom-Tom, Tambourine and Chinese Wood Drum

Easy to Maintain Given a small bit of your floor space the Link requires but little attention from you to be about its work of gathering nickels. The dropping of each coin starts the motor. The motor starts the vacuum pump and the roll. Each piece is ready for the next customer when the preceding piece stops. A little oiling and dusting keeps it even tempered and industrious.

Small Investment Required In even poorly located stores the Link proves an excellent investment. An average of $50.00 a month is a very common thing, $50.00 a week is not extraordinary.

Terms can be arranged so that the instrument not only pays for itself, but you are actually making money on it while paying for it. On request we shall be glad to furnish you with names of Link owners in your vicinity, and let them tell you what the Link will do.

The LINK piano is perhaps most famous for what followed it — the LINK aviation flight trainer, a device well known to all aviators. It combines player piano mechanisms and aviation components to simulate the actions of an airplane, and is particularly useful in training for instrument flight. The Link pianos were best known for their unusual system of playing the music, wherein the paper is dumped into one end and pulled from the other end of a bin, rather than being tightly wound between two spools.

somewhat different field. The LINK Piano Company of Binghamton, New York, was active not only in the construction of coin pianos, but theatre organs as well. Edwin A. Link, the son of the owner, was obliged as a young man to assist in the factory and in the erection of the pipe organs, but his real love was in aviation. When the piano and organ business collapsed along wih the stock market, young Ed tried a variety of ways to make a living in flying. His big success came when he developed a sort of imitation airplane for use in amusement parks. It resembled an actual airplane, and through various motions produced by mechanical bellows formerly employed in player pianos and organs, it actually simulated the real thing. Not that this carnival device was any great seller, but it lead to the development of the famous LINK trainer for the schooling of pilots in the intricacies of blind, or instrument, flying.

These devices were a tremendous asset in World War 2 when thousands of pilots had to be trained in a hurry, and today every aviator gets some schooling on this type of device. Thus it may be said that the great flight simulation industry of today owes a real debt to its forebear, the automatic piano! As a matter of fact, the early trainers were just about half airplane and half player piano . . .

Flight is simulated when student, enclosed under canopy, uses instruments to maneuver the Link on its swivel mount. Needle on instructor's desk records the Link's action.

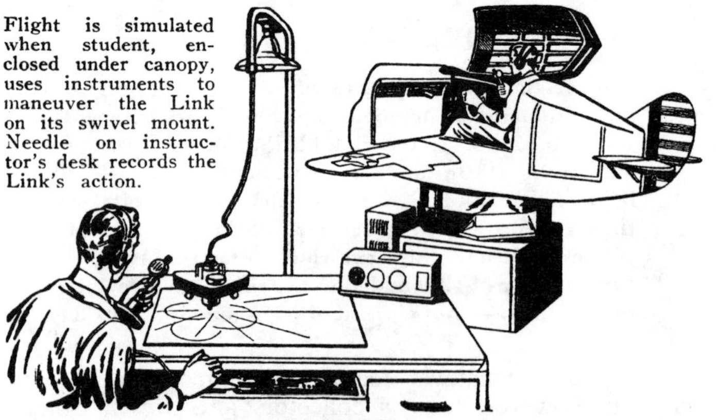

LINK TRAINER

Link made a variety of models of coin pianos, all of which featured the endless music roll wherein instead of being tightly wound on a spool, the music is dumped into one end of a sort of tub and withdrawn from the other end. This device eliminated the need for a rewind mechanism, but only at the expense of a more or less difficult job of

Violano-Virtuoso
Home Model

The most incredible of all the mechanically played instruments was the Mills Violano-Virtuoso, and the advertising campaign waged by its promoters was no less fantastic. While most of the machines were sold to Greek restaurant and candy-kitchen owners, valiant attempts were made to place it in homes such as is shown in the sketch above where a singer entertains her friends to the accompaniment of what even today is considered truly a remarkable mechanism.

changing the 15-tune rolls. While no trick for an expert, its difficult to imagine that many saloon-keepers had the patience to change their Link piano's music very frequently!

Of all the doo-dads, the gimmicks, and the gadgets that appeared during the thirty years of popularity of the coin-operated piano and orchestrion in America, no one will dispute the fact that greatest device from the standpoint of sheer technical excellence was the Violano-Virtuoso — the violin-playing machine manufactured and marketed by the Mills Novelty Company of Chicago.

This incredible apparatus was not the only attempt at mechanical playing of that most difficult of instruments, the violin, as Hupfeld of Germany had considerable success with a three-violined model, and there was also a French development along these lines. But the Mills Company was knowledgable in matters of marketing, and in the period from 1910 to 1929 they succeeded in placing between four and five thousand of these machines in public places! For some reason that is not clear, Greek restauranteurs and candy-kitchen owners had a particular affinity for the Violano-Virtuoso, and of the several hundred which survive today, a great many can be traced to this type of original ownership.

The Mills Company made its name in the building and selling of coin-operated gambling devices of a wide variety, the best known of which are the "one armed bandit" or "lemon, cherry, and bell-fruit-gum" machines. The intricacies of these pieces of apparatus made Mills a natural to take on the production of the violin machine perfected by Henry K. Sandell in the early years of the 20th Century. Sandell was, like Seeburg, a Swedish immigrant, but his forté was electricity and by the time he died in 1947, this self-taught electrical wizard had over 300 patents to his name!

While references to the Violano are found as early as 1905, evidently some years were spent in developing the market before Mills took on the project. The big event that helped push it over was the 1909 Alaska-Yukon-Pacific exhibition in Seattle, where the United States Government, in its Department of Commerce display, saw fit to show eight recent inventions which were intended to portray the technical progress of the nation. Seven of them were quickly forgotten, but Mills made sure that no-one ever forgot that the eighth one was the Violano-Virtuoso!

Forever after, each Violano-Virtuoso had prominently displayed in its lighted case a sign loudly stating that this invention was "Proclaimed by the United States Government as One of the Eight Greatest Inventions of the Decade." That isn't *quite* what the Government said, but it was close enough for Mills' purpose, and it certainly helped to keep the Chicago factory busy for the next 20 years!

There were two factors which permitted the success of the Violano-Virtuoso from a technical standpoint. One was the scheme whereby the strings are held taut not by pegs in the neck of the instrument, as in the case of a

The Mills Novelty Company of Chicago built between four and five thousand of these violin playing machines; this model sold for $2,500 in 1925, a huge sum in those days. Several hundred are still in playing condition in various collections and museums around the land.

Action Finishing and Tuning

The manufacture of the Violano-Virtuoso was a production-line proposition at the Mills factory. Mills was most famous for its line of gambling machines, notable among which was a complete series of "One-armed bandits" which today are almost completely outlawed in the United States save the State of Nevada and a few other isolated areas.

conventional violin, but by hanging weights which could easily be adjusted to change the tension of each string. Once adjusted, the strings were thus enabled to stay in tune indefinitely. The other factor was the bow. The bows of the violano are comprised of stacks of thin celluloid discs about the diameter of a 25¢ piece, totalling about a quarter inch in thickness. There is one bow for each string, mounted on a revolving shaft. When instructed by the music roll, the bow touches the string through a magnetic control, and the string is vibrated, just as it would be by the horsehair bow of a human violinist.

There is a chemical relationship between horsehair, cellulose, and celluloid, and it is said that this is the main realization that Sandell made which enabled him to go ahead and perfect the entire instrument.

Unlike most mechanical pianos, the Violano-Virtuoso works entirely by electricity, and its 44 piano notes are operated by solenoids. It can be seen in the pictures that the piano strings are arranged with the longest ones in the center of the piano frame; this feature enables the tension of the strings to be evened and supposedly the piano will thus stay in tune longer than it otherwise might. This set-up sure can drive a piano tuner out of his mind, however!

Roll Making Machines Busily At Work

The Children's Party

"THE reason why boys and girls leave home," once said a keen observer, "is that so few homes are made interesting for young people. The natural craving for amusement very often overcomes personal attachments."

Will you admit that you cannot give your children better reason to pass their evenings with you than to seek elsewhere for an outlet for youthful spirits? If you have sought for means to make your home attractive and have failed to solve the problem, why not provide music? Then there will be a source of constant interest and enjoyment for the young people.

And there is still another important reason why you should have such an instrument—it will develop the finer instincts in minds which are most receptive to influence. It will cultivate perceptions and create and enlarge ideals which might otherwise never become matured.

You can buy a piano or a violin, but consider that it will be years before a child can play either of them well, and then only if practice has been a daily duty regularly performed. Why should you spend money for music lessons, and why should the satisfaction of enjoying the best playing of the best compositions be deferred when you can have at once, more than years of practice can give?

Look back upon your own childhood and think what it would have meant to you then if you could have had such a means of recreation. Consider how satisfying it would have been for you to learn while still young, all the fine points of musical literature? Do you know them even now?

If you had to sacrifice the advantages now available with these instruments, see that your children have them.

At the Restaurant

THE manager of a famous restaurant once said "We have the best chef money can get, we have an unsurpassed variety of food, competent service, and a richly decorated dining-room; and yet, if we did not supply entertainment for our patrons our business would fall off to half what it now is."

Witness the efforts of prominent places to attract people and you will find that music is the one thing always first thought of and employed. The argument, then, is not whether music should or should not be used. The decision is to be made on the best and most economical means for providing it. Orchestras can be hired, but they will work only at certain hours; they do not always play well enough to please very critical people, and they make an expense which is a large item on the wrong side of the yearly statement.

Save an Unnecessary Cost

Why not take the cost of orchestra help (if not put into dividends) to decorate the room, to add rare dishes to the menu, or to improve the service? A Violano-Virtuoso, a Viol-Cello or a Viol-Xylophone will "let the musicians out" and will soon be paid for by the saving.

The very novelty of such an instrument is an advertisement. Those who hear its marvelous playing will mention it to others and the discussion which will follow will fix the name of the restaurant in their minds and associate it with up-to-date methods.

People who come at first out of curiosity will come again because the tones of these violins are so much more pleasing and so much more out of the ordinary than the effects of any other instrument or group of instruments.

The Automatic Cello was a valiant attempt to market a machine just one step greater than the Violano-Virtuoso, but it was not successful. Does anyone know of a surviving example of this most interesting apparatus?

The Encore automatic banjo is considered a prize collector's item today. Like the Violano-Virtuoso, it was promoted for home use as well as for playing in public places.

When properly adjusted and regulated, the Violano can be a marvelous sounding instrument, and it is regrettable that all too frequently the surviving examples are not put into this condition where they can be truly enjoyed by those privileged to listen to them.

Variations of the Violano-Virtuoso included the Viol-Xylophone (a violin accompanied by a xylophone), the Automatic Cello (as seen in the pictures on the opposite page), and the String Quartet. As far as is known, there are no surviving examples of any of these — but automatic instruments have a way of coming out of hiding places, and it may just be that some day we may once again have the opportunity of hearing one of these musical and mechanical marvels of a by-gone age!

Likewise, the Banjorchestra shown below is unknown today by any surviving examples, and this seems odd in view of the fact that considerable publicity accompanied its introduction in 1915. The Encore Automatic Banjo at the left was quite popular in its day, and its rarity is often ascribed to the fact that it was seldom sold outright, but was generally placed on "location" on a leasing arrangement by its owners — who were quick to withdraw the instrument when public interest waned. The Banjorchestra appears to be a combination of the elements of the Encore machine and one of the earliest piano frames as used in some of Henry K. Sandell's early Automatic Virtuosa models; it certainly must have been a delight to those who had the opportunity to hear it when first perfected!

The Automatic Marvel of the Age

The BANJORCHESTRA

THE USE OF THE BANJORCHESTRA

The Banjorchestra is a highly artistic automatic instrument which may be used in the place of the banjo orchestra, which has become popular in dancing salons, owing to its adaptability to the dance music of the day. Perfect rhythm for the modern dances has been worked out in the music rolls by which this instrument is operated. All the expression which is put into the music by the most extensive banjo orchestra is reproduced by this instrument. It may be used with great effect in high class dancing salons, and where cabaret entertainment is in vogue, and dancing is indulged in by the guests, at a saving of from $100 to $400 a week.

The Banjorchestra may also be used in ice-cream parlors, cafes and places of amusement as a coin operated instrument for profit.

6 ft. 7 in. high, 3 ft. 9 in. wide, 2 ft. 7 in. deep.

ACCESSIBILITY FOR REGULATION

All the controls are directly in front of the lower part of the instrument. The banjo is regulation size and equipped with wire strings. It may be tuned easily, by the use of four buttons which have been installed in the panel at the top of the instrument which sound the four notes of the piano to which the banjo should be tuned. The entire back of the instrument opens, so that the piano may be tuned with the greatest ease. By pressing a series of five buttons the traps may be cut off singly or as a group.

MUSIC ROLLS

Owing to their equipment and many years' experience as manufacturers of high-grade music rolls, the Connorized Music Co. is admirably well fitted to produce music rolls of artistic and attractive arrangement. Those for the Banjorchestra are specially prepared for dancing. The rhythm, expression and time which are all cut in the roll have been carefully and scientifically produced so that the greatest effect for dancing is had at all times. They have been cut and timed the proper length of the dance, and when rerolled commence over again for an encore. In fact, the Banjorchestra does what human hands have been doing at about one-tenth the cost.

Special rolls have been prepared for the Banjorchestra when used as a coin-operated instrument. Each roll comprises ten selections of the latest and most popular song and dance hits.

Banjorchestra—Showing Accessibility for Tuning

WHAT IT COMPRISES

The Banjorchestra comprises an automatic banjo supported by tambourine, triangle, bass and kettle drums and castanets, accompanied by an automatic piano. It is operated by an electric motor which may be attached to any ordinary electric socket, either alternating or direct current. It may be operated with or without a coin. If operated with a coin as many as 20 coins may be inserted at one time, and the instrument will continue to play until the last coin has been used. Its case design is highly artistic. It is finished in mahogany and the banjo and traps may be seen through a large plate-glass in the upper door. It is equipped with an automatic rerolling device, automatic expression devices for the piano, and an automatic muffler for the banjo.

PIANO MERCHANTS

should investigate our liberal proposition, and share in the profits of this 20th-century marvel.

The CONNORIZED MUSIC CO. 144th St. and Austin Place NEW YORK

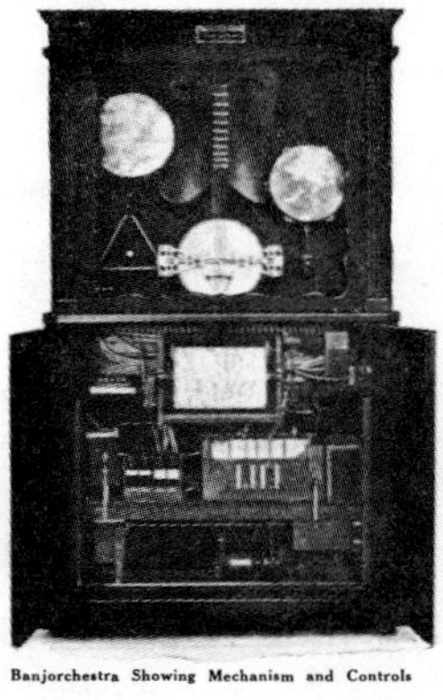

Banjorchestra Showing Mechanism and Controls

The Banjorchestra was first promoted in 1915, and articles in the trade papers hailed it as a truly great achievement. As this book is written no surviving examples have presented themselves, but it can be hoped that eventually one will turn up someplace so that modern-day enthusiasts for mechanical music can hear what sounds emanate from this interesting combination of piano, banjo, tambourine, triangle, bass and kettle drums and castanets!

COINOLA

Offers You Business that's always good. More Profit for your time than any line you sell. Freedom from worry and expense.

For 20 years they have stood every test and proven

The Best.

STYLE C Xylophone Exterior

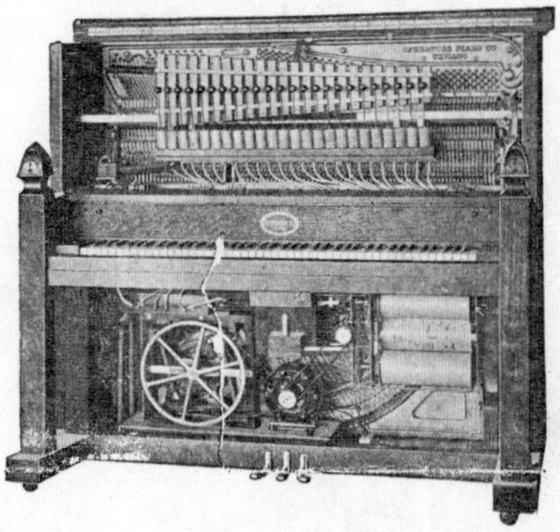

STYLE C Xylophone Interior

Simplicity of Construction

The reason they are so universaly in demand.

Durability of Parts

Assures absolute satisfaction Trouble-Proof operation and good music.

DON'T GUESS

You know you're right with a COINOLA.

STYLE C-2 Interior

YOU can make money with Pianos that satisfy.

COINOLA'S have satisfied for 20 years.

Sell one—Sell them always

There's a Reason

Your first COINOLA will show you why.

STYLE X Exterior

Where Quality Service Profits and Permanence are Appreciated You'll find COINOLA'S PROVE IT

STYLE X Interior

THE OPERATORS' PIANO CO.

715 North Kedzie Ave. Chicago, Illinois

Of all the automatic pianos presented to the public during the hey-day of this type of machine, none were more capable of delightful musical output than the Coinola line. The Operators' Piano Company seems to have made a specialty of having outstanding musical arrangements cut into the paper rolls which played on their instruments, and virtually all serious historians concede this point today. For some reason the manufacturers never made a point of this in their advertising, however, and it's fair to suggest that in neglecting to press this aspect of their efforts they missed a mighty good sales point.

Just how it relates to the company name is not clear, but when automatic pianos were popular, the concerns which placed "routes" of them in saloons and other places of public entertainment were known as "operators".

The artists at the Union Bank Note Company took time off from engraving stock certificates to come up with this delightful sketch of curious musicians trying to find the source of the music in this Berry-Wood orchestrion. Can it be that this new mechanical marvel has just thrown them out of work, as is suggested by many ads for these machines?

The Style CO Coinola is considered a real collector's prize today, with its magnificent case, beautiful art glass, and ability to use some of the finest music rolls ever cut — the famous style "O" rolls. These were used on Coinola instruments exclusively.

The Berry-Wood Piano Player Company
INCORPORATED

Style A. O. W.
In Rewind Music Only

CONTAINS Celebrated Berry-Wood Rewind Player. Case six feet high, ordinary width. Mission Design and Finish. Beautiful Art Glass Panels and Lamps. Has Thirty-four wood Flute Pipes, Thirty-four Violin Pipes, Coupler giving Ninety-two Pipe Tones. Twenty-five Steel Bells, Twenty-five Bar Xylophone, Kettle Drum, Castinets, Crash Cymbal, Triangle, Bass and Snare Drum, Cymbal, Device for drumming on rim; also Tambourine and Mandolin. Equivalent to a ten piece orchestra.

FACTORIES & OFFICES
348 to 50 Canal Place New York City
20th Street and Southwest Boulevard Kansas City

The Berry-Wood Piano Player Company was a very early factor in this field, and went out of business prior to the 1920's. Their instruments, consequently, are scarce today. Note that the model pictured above is the same one entertaining the musicians in the sketch at the upper left.

Unlike their European counterpart, the typical American orchestrion is a noise-maker rather than a device for true simulation of a real orchestra. While those who enjoy them are genuinely thrilled by the combinations of snare drums, bass drums, wood blocks, violin pipes, flute pipes, castanets, xylophones, glockenspiels, cymbals, triangles, and what-have-you accompanying the piano which forms the basic musical and structural framework of the instrument, it would be hard to argue that music in the classical sense is the result!

On the other hand, it can be said that the American orchestrion as represented by the machines built by Link, Coinola, Berry-Wood, Seeburg, North Tonawanda, WurliTzer, Western Electric, Chicago Electric, Peerless and the others are a true art form, permitting the production of a type of music not attainable by other means. And when

one considers that the elaborate cases with their beautiful art-glass fronts designed to attract as much attention as possible as they stood ready to accept the coins of all comers without regard to race, creed, or color, it is certainly true that nothing since has ever equalled their inherent and characteristic beauty. With designers eager to out-do each other in clever use of quartered-oak and mahogany veneers to enhance the musical outpourings of their innards, the results were truly the mechanical and artistic masterpieces of their day.

Colorful plastics and bright chrome-plate and stainless steel may inherit the Earth, but it seems unlikely that the gaudy juke-boxes of the mid-twentieth century will ever inherit the love and affection that owners of the surviving orchestrions of the 1920's place upon their machines from a day when life was a bit slower, a bit simpler, and perhaps even a bit more fun.

The Style LX at the left was the last of a series of orchestrions built by WurliTzer. The L refers to the case design; the X means it had an automatic roll changer as illustrated on a previous page. No self-respecting saloon of the period prior to the Volstead act would be found without its automatic piano or orchestrion. In the Chicago establishment below, the proud bartender stands ready to draw beers for all comers who are pulled from the street by the attraction of the sounds emanating from the Seeburg Style G shown just beyond the telephone booth. Between the tile floor, the pressed-metal ceiling, the art glass in the swinging doors, the polished spittoons all ready for action in front of the shiny mahogany bar of incredible length and the Seeburg orchestrion, this spot is a joy to behold!

Some Survivors of A Golden Age

L to r, top row: WurliTzer 146A band organ (p. 31), Autopiano (p. 13), Wilcox and White "self-playing orchestra" (p. 4). Lower row, Cremona Style G (p. 36), closed and open; Swiss cylinder-box with bells and drum. All machines on this and the next three pages are from the Author's collection. Page numbers refer to the text. All photos by John J. Young, Jr.

Top row, l to r: Link Style C closed and open, Mills Violano-Virtuoso (p. 39). Center row: Seeburg Style L (p. 37), Seeburg Style G closed and open (p. 44). Bottom row: WurliTzer Model CX closed and open, Bremond interchangeable-cylinder music box.

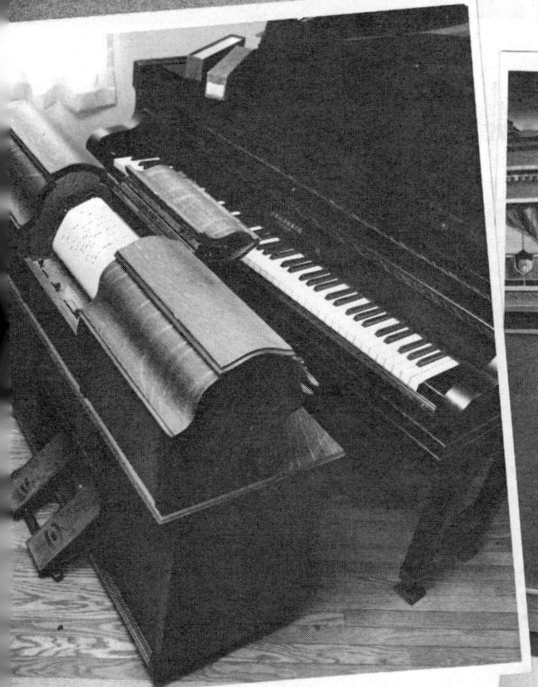

Top Row: Seeburg K. T. Special closed and open, Symphonion double-comb music box. Center row: Style 25 American Fotoplayer, Seeburg Style E piano, Gavioli 57-key Fairground Organ. Bottom row: Sterling "push-up" player, North Tonawanda Pianolin, Regina Automatic Concerto.

Top row: Reproduco piano-pipe organ, closed and open (p. 35), author's music hall entrance. Center row: Marshall and Wendell Model "B" Ampico reproducing piano, Steinway Model XR Duo-Art reproducing piano, 15 1/2" Regina single-comb music box. Bottom row: North Tonawanda Model 192 military band (p. 31), Julius Bauer Welte-Licensee reproducing piano, WurliTzer automatic harp.